A GRIM ALMANAC OF

HAMPSHIRE

JOHN VAN DER KISTE

A GRIM ALMANAC OF

HAMPSHIRE

JOHN VAN DER KISTE

The
History
Press

First published 2011

The History Press
The Mill, Brimscombe Port
Stroud, Gloucestershire, GL5 2QG
www.thehistorypress.co.uk

British Library Cataloguing in Publication Data.
A catalogue record for this book is available from the British
Library.

ISBN 978 0 7524 5489 4

Typesetting and origination by The History Press
Printed in Great Britain
Manufacturing managed by Jellyfish Print Solutions Ltd

CONTENTS

ALSO BY THE AUTHOR

A Divided Kingdom
A Grim Almanac of Cornwall
A Grim Almanac of Devon
Berkshire Murders
Childhood at Court 1819–1914
Cornish Murders (with Nicola Sly)
Cornwall's Own
Crowns in a Changing World
Dearest Affie (with Bee Jordaan)
Dearest Vicky, Darling Fritz
Daughter and the German Emperor
Devon Murders
Devonshire's Own
Edward VII's Children
Emperor Francis Joseph
Frederick III
George V's Children
George III's Children
Gilbert & Sullivan's Christmas

Kaiser Wilhelm II
King George II and Queen Caroline
Kings of the Hellenes
More Cornish Murders (with Nicola Sly)
More Somerset Murders (with Nicola Sly)
Northern Crowns
Once a Grand Duchess (with Coryne Hall)
Plymouth History & Guide
Princess Victoria Melita
Queen Victoria's Children
Somerset Murders (with Nicola Sly)
Sons, Servants and Statesmen
Surrey Murders
The Georgian Princesses
The Romanovs 1818–1959
West Country Murders
William and Mary
Windsor and Habsburg

INTRODUCTION & ACKNOWLEDGEMENTS

Hampshire and the Isle of Wight have a rich chronicle of dark history to compare with that of any other English county. Murders, suicides, fatal accidents, shipwrecks, air crashes, fires, epidemics, civil disturbances, and severe weather disasters have all taken their toll on the less fortunate. At least four events, namely the death of King William II (Rufus) in the New Forest in 1100, the sinking of King Henry VIII's flagship the *Mary Rose* in 1545, the assassination of the Duke of Buckingham at Portsmouth in 1628 and the defeated Duke of Monmouth's escape to Ringwood prior to his capture and execution in 1685, have long since become part of the nation's history. Ghost stories, superstition, and witchcraft have also featured in Hampshire's past. All these and more appear in the pages that follow, and I hope this journey through the ages will prove as rewarding to those who read it as it was to myself while researching and writing the pages that follow.

In doing so I have had the benefit of a variety of books, journals and websites. I would also like to acknowledge the help of Diane Webb, and of James and Hannah Cosgrave, for their help with photographing various locations; and of Nicola Sly, and Paul and Mary Wonnacott, for the loan of material. Last but not least, as ever, my wife Kim has been invaluable in her constant support and encouragement from the start of writing through to the reading of the final manuscript, as well as being ever ready to help with the photography, while my editors at The History Press, Matilda Richards, Cate Ludlow and Declan Flynn, have helped to see the work through to publication. My thanks are due to all.

Every reasonable effort has been made to obtain permission to reuse material which may be in copyright. I would be grateful if any owners whose rights may have been inadvertently infringed would notify us, so that an amendment can be made in subsequent editions.

John Van der Kiste, 2011

JANUARY

Ryde, where Charles Alexander, a surgeon, was arrested after a night
on the tiles on 24 January 1894.

Unfortunate cab-driver William Spriggs was killed in January 1860
after driving over his own neck.

1 JANUARY

Newbury Street, Whitchurch, one of the towns to send a fire brigade when Hurstbourne House caught fire in January 1891.

1891 Hurstbourne House, the seat of the Earl of Portsmouth, was destroyed by fire. At about 8.30 p.m. a servant smelt burning, and at the same time a woman passing by saw a glow in one of the windows. The flames spread quickly, and fire brigades were summoned from Andover, Whitchurch, and Basingstoke. Owing to the state of the frozen roads, they were delayed in arriving, and the available water was inadequate. The fire burnt itself out early the next morning, but little was left apart from the walls. The library of 5,000 books and most of the furniture were saved, but several works of art, including a portrait of Sir Isaac Newton by Godfrey Kneller, other portraits by Sir Joshua Reynolds and Anthony Van Dyck, and a priceless collection of Newton manuscripts all perished, as did the chapel adjoining the house. The family

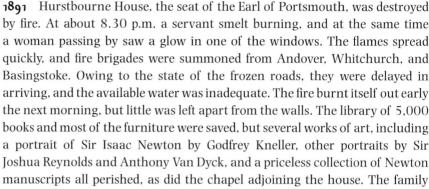

were away at the time, spending Christmas and the New Year in Devonshire. Arson may have been the cause; it was rumoured that a man had been seen behaving suspiciously in the grounds earlier that week, and on 29 December the brewhouse was reported to have been on fire (though the flames were soon extinguished by the servants). Later that year the family planned to rebuild the house on a smaller scale.

2 JANUARY

1817 When James Aldridge, of Wellow, near Romsey, came to check his dairy house, he found that he had been burgled overnight. The thieves had stolen a greatcoat as well as a large quantity of butter and cheese, and then helped themselves to various other provisions from the house before leaving.

3 JANUARY

Horndean, scene of a fire in which Edward Burton killed his wife Florence and himself in January 1933.

1933 Edward Burton (48) was a school attendance officer employed by Hampshire County Council and prominent member of the local British Legion. He and his wife Florence (47) were both found dead after a fire which destroyed Rosebank, a bungalow at Horndean, early in the morning. On the previous day he had sent his sister-in-law and housekeeper, Rosamund Bullworthy, and daughter Rose (9) to London for a short holiday. Residents were awakened by the roar and crackling of flames shortly after 2 a.m. It was a stormy night, and the Havant fire brigade arrived about twenty minutes later, but were unable to quell the flames and the bungalow soon burnt to the ground. When the

ruins were searched his body was found in a room at the front of the house, and hers in the kitchen. An employee at a local garage reported that Burton had bought two gallons of paraffin from him the day before, saying he needed them for cleaning.

At the inquest at Horndean on 6 January, it was stated that Burton had suffered from serious heart trouble, and he had never made a full recovery from a serious car accident in which he was involved six months previously.

He was also worried by the physical and mental health of his wife, who had spent some years in an asylum. Since her discharge she lived by herself, spent most of the day in the room in which she slept at night, and never spoke unless she was spoken to. He had written and sent a number of farewell letters dated 2 January, including one to the superintendent school attendance officer, thanking him for his kindness, saying he was leaving his service that day, that 'his troubles were purely private', and that he would rather they remained that way. He then shot his wife and himself dead with a Webley revolver which was found in a passage close to where his body was found. The empty tin of paraffin was also recovered. A verdict of wilful murder and suicide while of unsound mind was recorded.

1909 Private Frederick Harvey of the 1st Coldstream Guards appeared at Aldershot Police Court, charged with having criminally assaulted Mrs Annie Grant on Christmas Eve in Alexandra Road, Farnborough. As he returned home that afternoon, Mr Grant heard a woman screaming and saw a soldier running away. He tried to stop him, but as the soldier resisted, he knocked him down. Mr Grant then realised with horror that it was his wife who was screaming. As he went to her assistance, Harvey escaped. He had left his cap, belt and stick behind, and when he returned to barracks without them on Christmas morning he was handed over to the civil authorities. In his defence he pleaded that he had been drinking rum for several hours and had no recollection of anything that had occurred. He was committed for trial at the next Winchester Assizes. **4 JANUARY**

1883 Patrick McQuilkin (38), a cab driver of St George's Square, Portsea, was charged with stealing a pair of shoes, worth 8s 6d, from Henry Bishop, bootmaker, of Commercial Road. He had entered the shop with his mother-in-law, and he took the shoes (which were hanging on a nail just inside the door) while she was trying on a pair of boots. Walking out of the shop, he was followed by an assistant, Mr Harrison, who took him to the police station. He was sentenced to one month's imprisonment with hard labour. **5 JANUARY**

1882 Mary Ann Geddes (41) of Chatham Row, North Street, Portsea, attempted to commit suicide by throwing herself in front of a tramway car in Edinburgh Road while she was very drunk. She appeared at Portsmouth Police Court on 14 January, and expressed contrition for her behaviour. After being warned by the magistrates that her actions almost amounted to attempted murder (as they would have had severe consequences for the passengers if she had succeeded), she was discharged to the care of her husband, from whom she had been separated but who had said he was willing to take her back. **6 JANUARY**

1865 William Harvey (35), a butcher, was killed just before midnight, on the St Denis level crossing of the London and South-Western Railway, about a mile from Portswood, Southampton. An inquest was held at the Portswood Hotel on 9 January, at which the coroner said he understood that Mr and Mrs Harvey were on the line in a donkey-cart, and the gate had been left open at the level crossing. **7 JANUARY**

Mrs Harvey was seriously injured and initially thought unlikely to recover. The jury then went to view the body of her husband, which was lying in a house at the village, and evidence was taken on their return. One of the witnesses, William Snellgrove, said he and his wife had been coming from a nearby village when he heard the sound of a train arriving; he saw it strike something on the line and continue without stopping. They went to take a look, and on their way they met the gatekeeper with a light. He asked them to come and help him. All three searched the area carefully, eventually finding the bodies of a man and woman lying in the ditch and pulling them out. By then the man was dead, but as the woman was still alive she was taken to Southampton Infirmary, suffering from a broken left thigh and severe injuries to the head and spine. The enquiry was adjourned until the following week, when a verdict of accidental death was returned.

8 JANUARY   1802   Thomas Drokin, an Irishman aged about 30, was executed on board HMS *Acasto*, moored off Portsmouth. At 9.45 a.m. he was brought to the platform, attended by a Roman Catholic priest and some comrades. After spending twenty minutes in prayer, he gave a signal to say he was ready to die. He acknowledged the justness of his sentence, which was for 'uttering mutinous expressions', and for throwing a bottle at an officer, though he was drunk at the time. He begged his shipmates to take his fate as a warning, to be particularly attentive in obeying their officers, and while on board never to drink to excess. To the clergyman who attended him he gave a guinea, and he left £40 for funeral expenses, before he was 'launched into eternity'. His body was brought ashore from the ship in a coffin, put into a hearse, attended by two mourning coaches, and taken to a burial ground in St Mary's Street.

9 JANUARY   1450   Adam Moleyns, Bishop of Chichester, and one of King Henry VI's chief advisers who had represented the sovereign on several diplomatic missions abroad, was lynched in Portsmouth by a group of soldiers. A force of about 2,500 men had been gathered to reinforce British troops in France during the

Portsmouth Garrison Church, formerly Chapel of Domus Dei, where Bishop Moleyns of Chichester was killed by discontented seamen in January 1450. (*Mary Evans Picture Library*)

Hundred Years' War. Bad weather prevented them from embarking for several weeks; bored and discontented, they raided several towns on the south coast. Moleyns was sent to pay them their outstanding wages in the hope of pacifying them. He was conducting a service at the chapel of Domus Dei, now the Royal Garrison Church, when a gang of naval seamen who were resentful at not having had their full pay and being provided with only limited provisions burst in, dragged him outside and beat him to death. The town was excommunicated, and remained so until 1508.

1929   The body of Vivian Messiter (57), who had been a sales representative for   **10 JANUARY** the Wolf's Head Oil Co. in Southampton, was found on the floor of his garage in Grove Street. Decomposition had already begun and his face had been almost completely eaten away by rats, so it was only possible to identify him from the clothes he was wearing, and from a door key in his jacket pocket. Identification was carried out by Mr Parrott, of Carlton Road, with whom Messiter had lodged for some time. The last time he had been seen alive was when he left his lodgings on 30 October 1928. At first it was thought that he had died from a gunshot wound, but the Home Office pathologist Sir Bernard Spilsbury carried out a post-mortem and found that he had been struck over the head with a hammer or some similar implement.

Police enquiries led to William Thomas, a motor mechanic, alias William Podmore, who had a long criminal record. He was about to serve six months' imprisonment for robbery in Manchester, followed by a similar sentence for stealing wage packets in Wiltshire. When released on 17 December 1929, he was arrested and charged with Messiter's murder. He had written fictitious receipts for sales of oil to non-existent companies and was paid by Messiter, who had only taken him on that week and then discovered his new employee's fraudulent behaviour. After an argument Podmore killed him, stole his gold dress watch, torn the receipts from the receipt book, and fled. Pleading not guilty, he was tried at Winchester Assizes on 3 March 1930 before Lord Chief Justice Lord Hewart. At the end of a six-day trial the jury retired for nearly ninety minutes and found him guilty. When asked if he had anything to say before sentence, he repeated that 'I know nothing whatever about it'. The Home Secretary refused to grant a reprieve, and the prisoner was hanged at Winchester on 22 April.

1910   The bodies of Sergeant Harry Cheeseman of the Royal Marine Artillery,   **11 JANUARY** and his sister-in-law Elvina Alice Ruby Lefevre, who had been living with him and his wife, were found on the shore near Eastney in the morning. At the inquest at Portsmouth on 13 January, a letter written by Elvina in August 1909 was produced, declaring her 'ardent love' for him. Another letter, written by Cheeseman just before they died, was also produced, saying 'Me and Ruby have loved each other for a long time. We have grown to be part of each other's lives. What we are about to do is at her request.' A verdict of wilful murder and suicide was returned.

12 JANUARY **1780** Hans Stanley, a prominent politician and government minister who was born and lived at Paultons, near Romsey, committed suicide. Elected Member of Parliament for Southampton in 1754, he represented the city until his death, as well as serving as a Lord of the Admiralty and holding diplomatic posts in Paris and St Petersburg, being Chargé d'Affaires in Paris for a short time. He was known to have been embittered and depressed by his failure to secure a senior government post. While on a visit to Earl Spencer at Althorp in January 1780 he went for a walk in the woods on his own, and 'in a sudden fit of frenzy' cut his throat with a penknife. His father had also died by his own hand, in 1734, when Hans was only twelve years old.

13 JANUARY **1885** Alice Marie Boyett, aged three months, the daughter of a grocer's porter of Buckland, Portsmouth, had always been a sickly baby. She was fed from a bottle, her mother being unable to suckle her as she had an abscess. Alice suffered from mild bronchitis, and was attended by Dr Maybury from 9 January. She seemed to be making a good recovery, and was put to bed on 12 January as usual. At 6.30 a.m. next morning Mrs Boyett woke and found her dead in the bed beside her and her father. Dr Maybury was sent for, and said he thought death was the result of suffocation, probably caused by one of the parents turning over during the night and lying on her.

At the inquest at the Palmerston Arms, Buckland, on 19 January the Portsmouth coroner, Mr T.A. Bramsdon, remarked that this was the ninth case of suffocation which had occurred since he took office less than a year previously, from the 'old and pernicious practice' of allowing a child to sleep with its parents. He considered it a serious matter that young life should be so sacrificed for a cause which might easily be averted without danger to the child in another form.

14 JANUARY **1890** William Charles Beckenham (16), a labourer, committed a 'criminal assault' (presumably rape or attempted rape) on Louisa Brows (10) at Holdenhurst, near Portsmouth. It was not his first time before the court for such an offence, and he was charged at Southampton Crown Court on 19 March and given five years' penal servitude.

15 JANUARY **1850** The 18-month-old son of Mr Giffard, a Romsey fruiterer, accidentally pulled a teapot, full of freshly made hot tea, over himself while it was on the hub of the fireplace. He was severely scalded, and died in agony the next day.

16 JANUARY **1850** An inquest was held at Fareham on Stephen Sanday, and it was found that he had been killed by a double-barrelled gun going off while he was unloading it. The contents had entered one side of his head and death was instantaneous.

1922 John Pulling (72), a shipwright pensioner, beat his wife to death with a hammer at their home in Leonard Road, Portsmouth, and then cut his own throat. He had sent a letter to the chief constable stating that he was mad and intended to kill her and then himself. When the police entered the premises next morning, they found the bodies lying in the kitchen, and a number of incoherently written letters lying on the table.

17 JANUARY

1869 William John Kimber, aged ten months, was put to bed with the rest of the family at their house at Hounsdown. The eldest child, Edith (11), took her seven siblings up to bed after their mother had undressed them. She carried a candle upstairs with her, and about two minutes after she came down, Mrs Kimber heard him scream in terror. She ran up directly and found the room full of smoke, the curtains and part of the bed in flames. She took the boy from the bed and ran out of doors with him for him to get some fresh air, as he had almost been suffocated. After she had called for help, the fire was put out. As she did not think his injuries were particularly serious, she did not call for a doctor that night, but put some linseed oil on the burns. Next day she sent for Dr Wiltshire, who reassured her that they were not life-threatening, and applied some ointment. He called every day, but William's condition gradually deteriorated and he died on 30 January.

18 JANUARY

At the inquest on 1 February, Mrs Kimber said that he had always been a sickly child. She had taken him to several doctors in Southampton, and Dr Wiltshire had told her he would not live long as he was gradually wasting away. He gave evidence that the child had burns around the mouth, chin and neck, but though the wounds were not unduly dangerous in themselves, the child was in such a weakly state that in his opinion they merely accelerated his demise. His passing was a result of 'his system being so weak that it could not bear the effects of the burning'.

1886 William May was knocked down in West Street, Fareham, by a horse and cart driven by William Gregory. When he heard him cry out in pain, Gregory stood up in the cart and pulled the horse up, but it was too late. May was already unconscious and died from abdominal injuries twenty-four hours later. An inquest at the Royal Oak on 22 January returned a verdict of accidental death. The coroner remarked that it was the duty of all pedestrians and drivers to take greater care in the street, but agreed that no blame could be attached to Mr Gregory.

19 JANUARY

1895 In the morning Henry Lea, of the firm Huntley & Palmer, was travelling on a steamer from Cowes to Southampton. While in conversation with a friend, he collapsed and died, apparently of a heart attack.

20 JANUARY

21 JANUARY   **1911** The body of Miss Hazel Brown was found decapitated on a railway line near her home at Brockenhurst. She had been suffering from tuberculosis of the glands of the neck and arms for some time, and had been attended by over fifty doctors. At the inquest two days later, a medical witness said that she would never have recovered. Before leaving home, she wrote a farewell letter in French on the back of a visiting card, bidding her father goodbye. A verdict of suicide during temporary insanity was recorded.

22 JANUARY   **1888** Shortly after 6 p.m. window curtains and furniture caught fire at the house of Robert Morrant, a shipwright, at Fratton, after a table and a paraffin lamp were knocked over by children while they were playing. Mrs Morrant's clothes caught fire; she suffered severe burns, and had to be taken to hospital for treatment.

23 JANUARY   **1821** Thomas Cambridge, a gunner in the Royal Marine Artillery, and three other soldiers were travelling to Gosport late at night when they were attacked by a party who took a belt and cap away from them, and ran into Mrs Fraker's house. When the soldiers knocked on the door and politely asked for the missing articles, a gun was fired several times from one of the windows. Cambridge was wounded. The soldiers went to the police, and the men in the house were arrested. When they appeared at Winchester Assizes in August, the soldiers admitted they had been drinking that evening. The others, mostly young women, said they had spent the evening at Mrs Fraker's house nearby. One of the prisoners was her son-in-law, George Yeoman. The women planned to go part of the way home with Yeoman's 70-year-old father, but as they left the house they alleged that they were insulted and knocked down by Cambridge and his group. The men, who came to their assistance and took the belt and cap away, found themselves involved in a scuffle, which led to the soldiers drawing their bayonets. Old Mr Yeoman and Charles Gill, one of the men in the house, were both wounded. The soldiers then forced their way into the house, but were driven back. Gill put some gravel stones into

Union Street, Ryde, where Charles Alexander's drunken exploits attracted attention one night in January 1894.

his rifle and fired out of the window several times, hoping the intruders would disperse. It was at this stage that Cambridge was injured, though not seriously.

The judge said it was unnecessary to call any other witnesses. He said that if the jury believed the evidence of the young women, whom he thought were telling the truth, rather than that of soldiers, who were evidently drunk, they should acquit the prisoners. The jury agreed, and the men walked free from court.

1894 Charles Alexander, a surgeon practising at John Street, Ryde, was charged at Newport Borough Police Court with assaulting the police while he was drunk and disorderly shortly after midnight earlier that week. He had been seen by Sergeant Eldridge wandering around Ryde and knocking on the door of Warburton's Hotel. When requested to leave, he knocked the sergeant's hat off. He told the Bench he had no recollection of the incident, and was fined 10s with 5s costs.

24 JANUARY

1860 Thomas Scammell, a private in the 11th Foot Regiment, was found dead in the Basingstoke Canal, near the pontoon bridge. At the inquest two days later at the Royal Hotel, Aldershot, Private Richard Slowson, of the Royal Engineers, said he was on duty at the bridge, and on moving the bridge with a hook to let a boat pass, the hook became entangled in the clothes of a man lying in the river. After he removed the body from the water, he saw that it must have been there for some time. Scammell had been seen on Monday 23 January, during the evening, very drunk, walking towards the canal. Although he was reported absent that evening, no more was heard of him until his body was discovered. An examination revealed no marks of violence. On returning a verdict of accidental drowning, the jury recommended that in order to prevent similar cases in future, the canal should be fenced on both sides near the bridge, assuming that it could be done without impeding navigation.

25 JANUARY

Basingstoke Canal, close to where Private Thomas Scammell was found dead in January 1860. (*The Yateley Society, 2010*)

Canal from Norris Bridge, Aldershot.

26 JANUARY   **1849**   Mary Ann Beveridge walked into the police station at Portsea and told the constable that she had strangled one of her children, her five-year-old son James. Two years earlier she had killed thirteen-month-old Thomas; she was put on trial, but acquitted on the grounds of insanity. Severe post-natal depression, failing eyesight, and a frequently drunken husband who kept a mistress, meant her lot was not a happy one. She went on trial a second time and was acquitted again, but the judge ordered that she be detained at Her Majesty's pleasure.

27 JANUARY   **1860**   An inquest was held at Farnborough on the body of William Spriggs, a cab driver, who was found dead at the edge of a pond near the Tumbledown Dick Inn, with his horse and cab nearby. It was thought that he had intended to drive through the pond, which was often used as a thoroughfare, but he must have been very tired, even half asleep, and fallen from his box to the ground. There were marks on his chin, thought to have been caused by the wheel passing over him. The jury's verdict was that he had accidentally fallen, and died from the rupture of blood vessels on the brain; they also said that the pond was in a dangerous condition, and ought to be fenced in order to prevent similar accidents in future.

28 JANUARY   **1956**   The body of Private John Hall Lister, a young soldier from Leeds, was found on a railway line near RAOC barracks, Hilsea. He had been on national service for only a week. A letter to his parents was found in his pocket, saying, 'I will never make a soldier. I hated every minute of last week.' He had also written that he was 'sick of being called names I wouldn't call my worst enemy, and I am sick of food I can't bear to look at. I just can't stand it any longer. I wish I were dead.' Allegations of bullying at the barracks were mentioned, but at the inquest three days later, the coroner said he had gone into the matter carefully and could find no evidence to support them. A verdict of suicide was returned.

George Welch and Charles Woodford, arrested for attempted murder at Southampton in January 1881. *(Illustrated Police News)*

1881   The *Illustrated Police News* reported a case heard at Winchester two days
previously in which George Welch, alias Theasby, and Charles Woodford, both
painters, were charged with wounding Vasey Brumfield, his wife Mary, and
Charles Goddard, who lived with them, with intent to murder, at Basset, near
Southampton on 15 November last. Mr Brumfield had just returned to the house
from Southampton, where he had been collecting the rents on his property. At
about 5.15 that evening Welch came to his door, saying, 'Master, I have got
a job of work for you.' Mr Brumfield said he did not want to do business just
then, but Welch insisted on coming indoors, though he was told he could not be
admitted. At this moment Woodford was seen under the window by Ann Fry, the
housekeeper. While trying to stop Welch from forcing his way in, Brumfield was
knocked unconscious by a violent blow to the head. After he had come round,
he managed to crawl outside, where he was hit on the head a second time. As
he got to his feet, Welch caught hold of him, saying, 'Come back with me, and
see if we cannot catch these fellows'. He was then hit a third time, and fell to the
ground, pulling Welch down with him.

Welch then got up and ran back to the house, while Brumfield
staggered away to look for help. His cries were heard by Goddard's stepson
George Ferrans, who went and fetched Goddard. The latter tried to seize Welch
outside the house, and was shot in the neck. Woodford had got into the house,
where he accosted Mrs Brumfield, and when she asked him what he wanted, he
told her he would kill them all. He fired at her, leaving her unconscious, with
part of a bullet left in her head which could not be removed by surgical means.

The men were caught, found guilty of malicious wounding and attempted
murder, and sentenced to twenty years' penal servitude. Mrs Brumfield died
of bronchitis that same morning, though her death had almost certainly been
hastened by the ordeal.

1843   James Kedger fell overboard in Southsea Harbour and was drowned.

1880   Elizabeth Trimby, aged 2½, was left in the care of her grandmother Sarah
Pitters, at her house in Wyke Terrace, Winchester. Mrs Pitters had just lit a fire,
and was going into the next room, leaving the child alone, when she heard
screaming. She ran back to find Elizabeth's clothing ablaze, extinguished the
flames and removed the child's clothing as fast as she could. Dr Richards was
called to treat the child's burns, but she died that evening, at 7.30 p.m.

FEBRUARY

Gosport High Street, where the Bell Tavern was the scene of an inquest following an accident on 10 February 1885. (© *Nicola Sly*)

1 FEBRUARY   **1869**   A wagon drawn by three horses belonging to Mr Hall, a brewer at Alton, after depositing a load of lime at the Anchor Inn, Lower Froyle, was returning to Alton. At the crossroads, Islington Lane end, the horses were frightened by the noise of a passing wagon and ran away. The horses were held by the under carter, William Brambley, and the head carter, Thomas Page. Brambley was thrown on the road and trampled, but his injuries were so serious that he was dead by the time his body was taken back to the Anchor Inn. Page clung to one of the other horses until he relinquished his hold out of sheer exhaustion; he was thrown to the ground and the wagon passed over him. Despite prompt medical attention, he was not expected to recover. The horses ran on to Alton for nearly a mile, where one of the horses fell, being likewise dragged along the ground and badly injured.

2 FEBRUARY   **1952**   Mrs Edith Charlotte Link (23), of Mansell Road, Liverpool, fell from the carriage of a moving train onto the line shortly after leaving Southampton station. At hospital her injuries were found to be so severe that her right leg had to be amputated below the knee, and she sued the British Transport Commission for damages. The case came to court in January 1955, and Mr Justice Slade in the Queen's Bench Division gave judgment against her, saying she was either thrown from the train or deliberately jumped out while it was in motion. She and her husband had attracted attention on account of their behaviour at the station. They entered a compartment, and after arguing about taking a suitcase to London, Mr Link left before the train started. His wife denied that she ever opened the door. A car attendant said in evidence that, after he had locked up, he saw the door open, and saw the complainant standing beside it, saying she 'needed fresh air'.

     Summing up, the judge remarked on 'her incredible folly in jumping from the train' and thus losing part of her leg. In the circumstances, all he could say was that he rejected her evidence and had to leave it at that. He was satisfied that she did not intend to kill herself, but he had a suspicion that the reason for her behaviour was that there had been a dispute between her

Southampton railway station, where Edith Link was seriously injured in February 1952.

and her husband as to whether, when he went abroad, she should leave the house in which she had been living with him. Her allegations against the Commission had failed, and he found judgment for them, with £78 costs.

1831   A fire broke out in a farmyard close to the turnpike gate near Fareham at about 1 a.m., and burned up a barley rick. There were about twenty more ricks in the yard, which would have been destroyed but for the help of neighbours, who rallied round to help. They called a fire engine, which put out the bonfire without any further damage being done. Two men seen in the town shortly afterwards, going into a pub to light their pipes, were thought to have been responsible, but they were never traced.

3 FEBRUARY

1916   Lieutenant Georges Codere (22), acting adjutant of the 41st (Montreal) Canadian Infantry at Bramshott Camp, went on trial at Winchester Assizes, charged with the murder of Sergeant Henry Ozanne on 8 December 1915 at Arundel House, Grayshott. He claimed Ozanne had seen him kill another man, and was afraid of being court-martialled. After an appearance before Alton magistrates just before Christmas, he was committed for trial. It was proved that he had financial problems, and evidence was produced to suggest that he was weak-minded, could not be trusted to follow orders, and was known in camp as 'le fou' (the madman). In Quebec he had been cautioned for driving through the streets too fast, to which his response had been, 'What does it matter if I do kill anybody?' During a car accident in October, shortly before coming to England, he had been thrown out of the vehicle, and it was said that he had behaved oddly ever since. He might have been insane at the time he battered his victim to death. The jury retired for twenty minutes and found him guilty. Mr Justice Darling sentenced him to hang, but an appeal was lodged, and this was commuted to deportation and life imprisonment in Canada.

4 FEBRUARY

1892   An inquest was held at Portsmouth on John Henry Knight, who had cut his throat. He had invested £400, his entire life savings, in the Portsea Island Building Society, and its failure had preyed much on his mind. A verdict of temporary insanity was recorded. Less than two years later, Mr Moses, a Portsmouth shipwright who had lost £300 of savings through similar circumstances, hanged himself in his garden.

   Established in 1846, the Society derived most of its support from 'naval officers, dockyard men, pensioners, and the most thrifty of the working classes'. After increasing difficulties it crashed in December 1891, and three months later criminal proceedings were launched against several directors and auditors for falsification of accounts and conspiracy to defraud.

5 FEBRUARY

1922   An inquest was held at Eastbourne on the body of Samuel Whetton (22), a monumental mason of Besting, Southsea, whose body had been found on the Crumbles. His father said that his son served in the trenches at the age of 17. As an officer he was wounded in France, but had never recovered from the shock. He had been missing from home since October 1921. In January he wrote to his

6 FEBRUARY

father asking for money, adding that he was 'fed up with the whole thing and am going to do myself in'. His father telegraphed £10 and went to Hastings, but found that his son had already left the town. Dr Adams, the police surgeon, said that death was due to the taking of nitrate of silver, an open packet of which was found on the body. A verdict of 'suicide while of unsound mind due to war service' was returned.

7 FEBRUARY

1895 George Buckle (60), who had lodgings at Marylebone Street, Southsea, and worked at the Bedford Hotel, was very much affected by the cold weather. He used to earn 6d a week, sometimes less, for pushing trucks around and general odd jobs. He and his wife received parish relief of 3s a week, of which 2s went on rent. In the evening he had a crust of bread and a cup of tea for supper, 'and talked very queerly'. Next morning his wife found him dead in bed beside her. The doctor attended the emaciated man, who had no nightshirt on; his only bedclothes were a few old coats and underclothing. An inquest was held at Winchester Assizes two days later.

8 FEBRUARY

1856 Thomas Jones, a prisoner on the convict hulk *Stirling Castle* in Portsmouth Harbour, serving six years' penal servitude for robbery, asked to see a doctor and had a consultation with the assistant surgeon, Charles Hope. He was suffering from chest pains and had been annoyed by being moved from the comfortable lower deck, with its better food and beds, to the middle deck, where prisoners received more meagre rations and slept in hammocks. Hope told him that he did not consider any treatment was necessary and refused to authorise Jones's return to the lower deck on the grounds that it was already overcrowded. An enraged Jones stabbed Hope to death with a home-made knife which he had carried around with him. It emerged that on the previous evening he had told the chaplain that he meant Hope to examine him again, and would give Hope 'another chance for his life'. Jones went on trial at Winchester Assizes on 6 March and was found guilty. He was executed by Thomas Calcraft on 22 March.

The arrival of the fleet at Portsmouth harbour, late seventeenth century.

1962 Denis Doyle (44), a caterer from Brighton, was sentenced at Winchester Assizes to three years' imprisonment for arson. After a nine-day trial he was found guilty of maliciously setting fire to the Picket Post Hotel, near Ringwood, with intent to defraud. On the direction of Mr Justice Barry, he was acquitted of setting fire to the hotel while his wife and four-year-old son were inside. Additional charges of fraud, to which Doyle had not been asked to plead, were allowed to remain on file, not to be proceeded with without authority.

9 FEBRUARY

1885 An inquest was held at the Bell Tavern, High Street, Gosport, on the body of Percival Ibbetson-Brown (10), who lived with his mother at Little Beach. He had been killed in a tramcar accident the previous evening. Alfred Gill, a newsboy, identified the body. At the time of the accident, Alfred had been with the deceased at the bottom of High Street, selling evening papers. A woman on the opposite side of the road called to them, and Gill ran across the tramway, closely followed by the deceased. Gill fell over in the middle of the road, and Ibbetson-Brown fell on top of him. A tramcar was approaching at 4mph, and the driver called to them to get out of the way. Gill moved in time, but his companion did not: he was run over, despite the driver's attempts to stop. In passing a verdict of accidental death, the jury recommended it would be advisable to place a guard around the tramcars, so in future nobody could go under the wheels.

10 FEBRUARY

A nineteenth-century impression of the Bell Tavern, Gosport, scene of an inquest in February 1885.

1880 Henry Dudman (63), a shepherd employed by Mr Barton of Pitt Farm, near Winchester, went to look after the ewes and lambs in his charge during the evening – for the last time. He had previously spoken to others of hanging himself, and next morning his body was found suspended from a hook in his shepherd's house. The inquest next day returned a verdict of temporary insanity.

11 FEBRUARY

1950 Mrs Lilian Berry (38), a widow, was staying with her sister, Mrs Massingham, at Kimberley Road, Eastley, Portsmouth. While she was in the scullery, a shot was fired. Her sister ran to see what had happened and found her lying on the floor with a bloody wound to the head. As a 999 call was being made, a second shot was heard from the yard behind the house. When the police arrived, they found John Allcock (30), of Brockley, south-east London, lying in the yard with a similar wound. Both were taken to hospital, but they died shortly after admission. An inquest on 15 February at Portsmouth returned a verdict of murder and suicide. It was thought that he had been courting her but she had rejected his advances, and he was seeking revenge.

12 FEBRUARY

1897 Elizabeth Franklin (26) threw the contents of a lighted lamp over Sarah Broomfield at Southampton. She appeared at Winchester Assizes on 2 July, charged with intent to cause grievous bodily harm. It emerged that Franklin

13 FEBRUARY

and her partner John Lahee had been lodging with Mr and Mrs Broomfield. After a quarrel Franklin threw the lamp at her, inflicting severe burns on the head and face. Neither she nor Lahee made any effort to put out the flames, and it was only thanks to the prompt action of a neighbour, George Blanchard – who had seen what was going on, broken through the window, and put the flames out – that she was not more seriously injured. The judge, Mr Justice Day, said he felt that Lahee should also have been charged. Franklin, whom he called 'a violent and dangerous woman', was sentenced to five years' penal servitude.

14 FEBRUARY   **1824**   According to the *Hampshire Telegraph & Times*, 'A creditable householder, of the parish of Nutshaling, near Southampton, of the name of Clarke, was summoned before the magistrates of Romsey, and fined £5 for the crime of setting a gin in his own garden, to protect his vegetables from the depredations of rabbits, hares, or other vermin. It appears, then, that a man may set a spring gun or traps in his grounds to catch a thief who shall violate the laws of property, but, by the Game Law, to set a gin to catch animals which daily destroy his property, is an offence.'

15 FEBRUARY   **1886**   An inquest was held at the Coffee Tavern, Nobb Lane, Portsmouth, on the body of an unnamed male child which had lived with its parents at St Mary's Street. The father, William Hearle, a licensed hawker, said the baby was born on 4 January, but had always been delicate and sickly, constantly throwing up its food. On the night of 11 February it was 'very troublesome', and the next morning the mother decided to take it to a doctor. She had got up and warmed some water with which to wash it, but on taking it up from the bed found it was dead. Dr Morley, who was called to see it, said it was very emaciated, small for its age, 'had a very old look about its countenance', and small sores on both ankles. Emaciation was due to want of proper food and nourishment. It also had thrush, which caused blood marks around the mouth.

Mr Hearle said the money he earned would not allow him to purchase more food. He only came into the town from Bath on Thursday, and had to remain at Gosport to sell three old umbrellas, as all the money they then had was 4*d*. He had not applied to the parish authorities. The coroner, Mr T.A. Bramsdon, said it was a painful case, but Dr Morley said he thought the mother had acted in ignorance. Mr Bramsden said it showed how in all large towns there was still a great deal of poverty. Mr Hearle said the last halfpenny had been spent on biscuits for the child, and they could only hope that by such cases becoming known, and with better trade, a repetition of them would be obviated.

16 FEBRUARY   **1860**   An inquest was held at Stockbridge on the body of Emma Mott (2), who had died in the town earlier that week from injuries caused after her clothes had caught fire during her mother's absence. Emma's mother had left Emma and her twin sister by themselves in the room with a fire burning in the hearth, and nothing to prevent them from coming too close. In reporting the case, a local newspaper regretted that, 'Hundreds of children are roasted alive from the same cause, but nothing will induce the parents to provide wire guards for their protection.'

1921   At Winchester Assizes Emily Matilda Perry was found guilty of the wilful murder of her son Edward John while insane. The judge ordered that she should be detained during His Majesty's pleasure.

1883   The Isle of Wight Co. steamer *Vectis* left Southampton at 2.30 p.m. While it was passing between Hythe and HMS *Hector* off Netley, a female passenger was seen to jump overboard from forward, near the wheel. The skipper immediately ordered the vessel to stop; the engines were reversed and the boat was lowered. The woman, the wife of a yacht captain at Southampton, asserted that she had tried to kill herself; she was picked up, attended to on board, and put ashore at Cowes, having suffered nothing worse than a thorough drenching. The officers and crew of *Vectis* were praised for their prompt action in having saved her life. When they arrived at Cowes, she was handed over to the police and summoned to appear before Ryde magistrates later that week.

1881   James Lay of Hillway Farm, Brading, near Ryde, was charged at Newport with cruelty to two horses. Frank Cotton, a postmaster who lived with his mother in Ryde, had made an arrangement with the defendant to take two horses to Hillway. An agreement was made whereby Lay would allow them to feed or graze in his fields in fine weather, and when it was rough he would put them under shelter, or give them corn indoors when it was very stormy. In mid-January, when he visited Brading, he saw that the horses did not look well, and neglected, and asked for them to be returned home. On 22 January, when there was thick snow on the ground, as they were being taken to Ryde, one was so weak and in such poor condition that it collapsed and had to be shot. The other was still recovering. Lay was fined £5 and £1 8*s* 6*d* costs.

1896   Frederick Burden (24), a labourer, had been living with Angelina Faithfull at Brooklyn Road, Portswood, Southampton, since Angelina had left her husband in December 1893. Both of them were heavy drinkers, and they were often heard quarrelling by neighbours. In the morning, Sarah Phillpot, a girl who lived nearby and used to run regular errands for Faithfull, called round to see them. As she found the front door locked, she made her way round to the back and found Faithfull lying dead in bed. The bedclothes and her garments were all covered in blood, and she had a razor in her right hand. There was a wooden bucket on the floor, full of bloodstained water, in which it was assumed her assailant must have washed his hands after committing the deed. Sarah immediately ran back to tell her mother, who alerted the police. Meanwhile ,Burden had walked towards Salisbury, making a point of calling at public houses in the town that evening to consult the local newspapers in each one so he could study the reports of Angelina's death. He was arrested and charged with her murder, as well as with putting the razor in her hand in an attempt to make her death look like a case of suicide.

The finding of the body of Angela Faithfull at her Southampton home in February 1896. *(Illustrated Police News)*

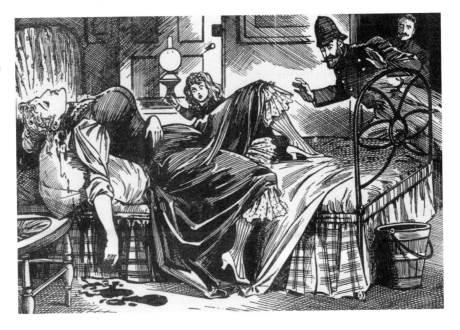

At the end of the first trial at Winchester Assizes on 29 June, the jury were unable to agree on a verdict; however, at a retrial on 1 July Burden was found guilty. A recommendation to mercy on account of his previous good character and youth was made. Nevertheless, he was sentenced to death, and was one of three convicted murderers to be hanged at the city gaol on 21 July 1896.

21 FEBRUARY **1917** The RMS *Mendi*, a Liverpool screw steamer carrying over 800 South African labourers and a few army officers to the Western Front in France with a destroyer as escort, was twelve miles south of St Catherine's Point when she collided in thick fog with the liner *Darro* shortly before 5 a.m. She had sailed from Cape Town on 16 January carrying 823 troops of the 5th Battalion,

St Catherine's Point lighthouse, close to the point where RMS *Mendi* collided with the liner *Darro* in February 1917.

South African Native Labour Corps, and stopped at Plymouth before leaving for her destination of Le Havre. Most men on board were on their way to dig trenches, carry stretchers, repair roads and carry out other manual labour, rather than fight. During the accident she was struck on her starboard side, near the foremast, keeled over and sank about twenty-five minutes later. The escort searchlight had failed due to poor visibility, with fog and darkness making an effective rescue impossible, and 625 men, mostly labourers, drowned or died of exposure and hypothermia in the icy waters. Various vessels nearby were able to rescue the survivors, and two officers, ten NCOs, and 191 South Africans were saved.

An inquiry was held in London five months later, and Captain Henry Stump of the *Darro* was held to be responsible for the wreck. He had been travelling at a high speed in thick fog, and admitted making no efforts to lower any of his boats in order to save the lives of those at risk. His captain's certificate was suspended for one year.

1856   William Ansell, a naval steward who had only recently returned to   **22 FEBRUARY**
England, and his wife Amelia, of Kettering Place, Mile End, Portsmouth, were heard quarrelling late at night. She loudly begged him to give her time to make her peace, and her plea was followed by a gunshot. A neighbour went into the house and found Amelia lying on the floor, bleeding, and although medical aid was summoned she died about an hour later. A six-barrelled Colt revolver with five barrels loaded was found on the premises. Her husband claimed that he had the pistol in his hand to frighten her, but that he did not know it was loaded until she touched it and thus caused it to go off. They had arranged to take possession of an inn the following week, so the theory of premeditated murder seemed unlikely, but he was committed for trial at the next Winchester Assizes. No report can be found of any proceedings, so it is likely that the case was either thrown out or else he was discharged.

1850   An inquest was held at the Bridge Tavern, Northam Road, Southampton,   **23 FEBRUARY**
on a child (whose gender was not specified) which had died after alleged ill-treatment. A surgeon who had attended it said it died from scarlatina. There were some marks of violence visible on the body, but no evidence to show how they had been caused. The jury returned a verdict of death from natural causes.

1855   Major Charles Young, of the Royal Horse Artillery, had just returned   **24 FEBRUARY**
from active service at the Crimea and was travelling from Turkey to rejoin his wife and family at Ryde. He broke his journey at Portsmouth, and decided to stay at the Fountain Hotel, where he fell from a top-storey front window sometime after 2 a.m. A surgeon, Mr Thomas Rolph, was called immediately, but Young died within two hours of being carried indoors. Captain Andrew Savage of the Royal Marine Artillery identified the body, and said the deceased had received a flesh wound in the trenches at Sebastopol. He did not know whether Young had suffered from fever as well, but had had a letter from him (they were hoping to meet later on that day). The fall had caused a ruptured vessel, and a verdict of accidental death was returned.

25 FEBRUARY   **1952**   Three men from Parkhurst Prison, Thomas Ward (32), Ronald Lawrence (29), and Patrick Culliney (36), were charged at the Guildhall, Newport, with intent to murder Richard Neville D'Arcy (48), a fellow prisoner. D'Arcy had been found in his cell at Parkhurst on 2 February with a 6in wound in his throat. The attack was apparently an act of revenge, as D'Arcy had recently procured the transfer of another prisoner to custody at Princetown, Devon.

At Winchester Assizes, on 18 March, Ward claimed that on 1 February he had said to D'Arcy, 'I suppose you are happy now. You had Jimmy Heaton sent to Dartmoor this morning.' D'Arcy denied that he had had anything to do with it. Next day, said Ward, at D'Arcy's cell door, the latter grabbed him by the shirt, pulled him forward and hit him with a jug, smashing his spectacles.

At the end of a two-day trial they were found not guilty of wounding with intent to murder, but convicted of wounding with intent to disfigure or cause grievous bodily harm. Ward was sentenced to five years' imprisonment, and the other two were each given four years, to follow the sentences they were currently serving.

26 FEBRUARY   **1814**   Mr Rolfe, an elderly painter, lived alone in Middlebrook Street, Winchester. One day he lit a fire in his room. Unfortunately, sparks flew out, and his clothes caught fire. He did not recover from the burns. At an inquest the coroner recorded a verdict of accidental death. Although he had often told his neighbours he lived in poverty, two guineas, and several bank notes, which 'were almost in pieces', were discovered when his rooms were searched.

27 FEBRUARY   **1882**   Robert Fisher (15), a black American, was charged at Southampton Magistrates' Court with the wilful murder of John Macaulay, mate on the barque *Voyageur*. According to the evidence of a Russian sailor, who spoke through an interpreter, Fisher came on board at Richmond, US, in November 1881, sailing for Pernambuco, South America. Throughout the voyage he was persistently bullied and teased by the captain and Macaulay, and made to undertake tasks which should have been done by the elder sailors. His temper gave way soon after midnight on 20 December, when he dropped a pot of grease on deck and it made a mess. An argument led to a struggle, and Fisher used a sheath knife (with which he was meant to clear up the grease) to stab his tormentor. Macaulay died within a few minutes and was buried at sea. When asked what he had done, Fisher said at first that he had been aloft, scraping the mast, and that the knife must have fallen from his pocket.

At Winchester Assizes, on 19 May, the jury found Fisher guilty of manslaughter, but with a strong recommendation to mercy on account of his age and the provocation to which he had been subjected. Mr Justice Hawkins gave him one month's imprisonment, during which, he said, he hoped Fisher's friends 'could arrange for his future well being'.

28 FEBRUARY   **1885**   James Hunt (53) of Winchester, began a new job as a cowman at the County Asylum, Knowle. His wife Ann saw him getting up at 4 a.m. on 2 March and asked if he would be back to breakfast at about 7 a.m. He said he did not know. It was the last time she ever saw him alive. Later that day the

asylum bailiff came to ask her why he had not arrived at work that day. She instinctively felt something was wrong, and reported the matter to the asylum authorities; they searched the river, and contacted the Winchester police, but without finding out anything. Next morning, another employee at the asylum discovered his body hanging from a tree in the local cemetery. At the inquest on 4 March, his widow said he had been badly injured in the head eighteen months earlier, after falling from a ladder, and frequently complained of pain. A verdict of suicide was recorded.

A GHOST AT WINCHESTER CATHEDRAL

In 1962 the wife of a former canon of Winchester Cathedral was said to have frequently seen the figure of a monk limping across a garden at the Close. It would pass through the wall and glide, still limping, into the cathedral. Later, when the wall was demolished, three skeletons were unearthed. According to

29 FEBRUARY

The west end of Winchester Cathedral, said to be haunted.

an archaeologist, who was familiar with the area, these remains were of men who had probably been members of a medieval monastic order. The bones of one suggested that he had suffered from arthritis, which could have explained why the ghostly apparition was limping. After the skeletons were reburied, the monk was never seen again.

Winchester Cathedral, showing the north transept and Norman arches.

MARCH

Fordingbridge, scene of a housebreaking in March 1861. (© *Nicola Sly*)

1 MARCH

1888 George Jackson (54), a merchant seaman, was charged at Southampton Borough Police Court with wilfully causing the death of Frederick Aldous (20), a native of Southampton, by stabbing him in the chest with a knife whilst he was on board the English barque *Emma G. Scammell*, at Bahia, Brazil, on 9 February. They had both joined the ship at Cardiff. It had discharged their cargo after they reached Brazil, and was lying at anchor when John Briggs, the first mate, gave the order for dinner. Jackson and Aldous were both standing near the galley, and an altercation arose between them as to who should carry the food. A scuffle ensued, during which Aldous was stabbed.

On 5 March, Jackson appeared at Winchester Assizes accused of murder. For the defence, Mr Giles said that, according to Jackson's statement, Aldous had rushed at Jackson whilst he had a sheath knife in his hand and was about to eat his dinner, and merely fell onto the blade. There had previously been an altercation between the two as to which of them should carry the dinner, and a Norwegian sailor said that he saw the prisoner holding the deceased down and biting his hair. The defence argued that there had been 'no offensive intention' on the prisoner's part: whatever wound may have been sustained was a result of the struggle begun by the deceased, who fell into a fit of rage when Jackson refused to carry in the dinner. In summing up, the judge told the jury that the case hung on a question of whether the death of the deceased was caused wilfully in the heat of the fight, in which case they must find a verdict of manslaughter, or whether the wound was the result of an accident, as suggested by the defence, in which case they would have to acquit the prisoner. As no evidence of premeditation was forthcoming, a capital charge could not be supported, the prosecution asked for the case to be withdrawn, and Jackson was discharged.

2 MARCH

1829 Samuel Langtrey, a frail, elderly retired bricklayer, and his housekeeper Charity Joliffe, were found beaten to death in their home at Prospect Row, Portsmouth. The house had been ransacked, and money and various items were found strewn around the floor, as if the killer had been disturbed and left in a hurry. A few days later, Langtrey's barber, John Stacey, who had shaved him twice every week (the last time on the day the old man was killed) was seen to be spending money rather freely. He was arrested on suspicion of murder. When he was searched, his clothes were found to be badly bloodstained. His father, also called John, was charged with being an accessory to the crime, and admitted to having dug up and reburied a large amount of money and a stolen watch which his son had brought back to the house; despite knowing that his son had committed the murders, he had said nothing to the authorities. Both men appeared at Winchester Assizes in July. John Stacey senior was acquitted, but his son was hanged on 3 August. The public had been so revolted by the crimes that there were suggestions that the Home Secretary should be petitioned to allow him to be publicly executed in front of the house where Langtrey and Joliffe had been killed.

1853 William Smith and George Perkins were charged at Winchester Assizes   3 MARCH
before Mr Justice Erle with attempting to murder Henry Biddlecombe at Boldre.
Biddlecombe was a gardener employed by Sir George Burrard at Walkhampton
Park, near Lymington, and lived in a small cottage adjoining the park. At about
1 a.m. on 30 December 1852, he was woken by a knock on the front door. When
he went to answer it the prisoners ran in, and when he resisted them he was
attacked about the head with a large stick. The two men had come to burgle
the premises, but although there were several gold sovereigns to be found, they
escaped with only a penny and a farthing. The jury found them guilty and they
were sentenced to transportation for life.

1867 Miss Wheeler brought an action against Mr Watts for assault and false   4 MARCH
imprisonment. On the death of her father, a coal merchant at Redbridge, near
Southampton, she had carried on the business for a while; she then sold it
to Mr Watts, on the understanding that she and her mother could continue
to occupy two rooms in the house. There had been some dispute between
Wheeler and Watts, which came to a head on 18 March 1865. She kept a
pistol beside her and was in the habit of firing it at random. When she did so
that morning, Watts thought he was aiming at him: he went to Southampton
Police Station, claimed he was 'in bodily fear of her', and obtained a warrant
against her. As she was undressing for bed that night, a policeman came to
arrest her and took her to the station. She was locked in a cell for two nights
and then taken before the magistrates, who dismissed the complaint. Watts
claimed she was 'exceedingly violent – almost mad' that morning, and would
have been capable of attacking him with her bare hands. She complained that
during her imprisonment she had been put in a common cell with a stone
floor, unfurnished except for a wooden bench, with only felons and vagabonds
for company. The jury returned a verdict on her behalf, and she was awarded
damages of £50.

1935 While aircraft from the RAF base in Gosport were operating off the   5 MARCH
eastern end of the Isle of Wight in the afternoon, an Osprey machine, piloted
by Sub-Lieutenant Nigel Radcliffe Williams, RN, with whom was Leading
Aircraftman Henry John Atkinson, fell into the sea. Williams was attached to
the Gosport base for instruction. HMS *Hood*, on her way from Portsmouth to
rejoin the fleet in the Mediterranean, saw the machine fall, stopped, and lowered
a boat which proceeded to the scene of the accident. When the boat arrived,
however, the machine had vanished beneath the waves. The body of Williams
was found floating in the sea and was landed later in the evening. Atkinson was
missing, presumed drowned.

1886 William Titheridge (10) broke into the house of William Blake Tickner   6 MARCH
at Saxe-Weimar Terrace, Albert Road, Southsea. Tickner locked his premises
at about 10.30 p.m., and came down the next morning to find the kitchen
window had been forced open. On searching, he discovered that somebody
had slept in the shed in the rear. He found some footprints in the snow, and
took a tracing. When Master Titheridge was apprehended, it was found that

these corresponded with his boots, particularly as one nail from the sole was missing. He had been away from his house at Edmond Road, Southsea, from 8 a.m. on Friday 5 March until the following night, when he was found at his grandfather's at Gosport. Sometimes he stayed out all night, and he had been regularly punished for it by his father. He already had a previous conviction for larceny and housebreaking at the same premises in December 1885, and at another house in the same area later that same month. On both occasions he had been sentenced to receive six strokes with a birch rod. He pleaded guilty and was sentenced to fourteen days' hard labour, followed by five years in a reformatory.

7 MARCH   **1923**   The mutilated body of Colonel Edward George Curtis, secretary of the Royal Naval Club, Portsmouth, was found on the railway. He had never really recovered from the effects of war service. He had left the club on the previous evening to go on leave. Earlier in the day, an old friend had received a letter from him saying that he was going 'to do away with himself', as he 'had been driven to it by worry', and mentioning where his body would be found. His friend thought this was purely imaginary, as all his affairs were in perfect order. A verdict of suicide while of unsound mind was returned at an inquest at Rowland Castle on 10 March.

8 MARCH   **1828**   Moses Sheppard (23) confessed to the murder of William Harmsworth. William's body was found lying in a ditch beside the turnpike road near Fareham on the evening of 22 December 1827. He had been repeatedly stabbed, one of his ears had been cut off, and his head had been almost severed from his body. A bricklayer at Gosport, Harmsworth had been a conscientious worker, and was one of the lucky few not to be laid off by his employer during the winter months when there was little work to be had. Other members of the workforce were jealous, and some of them sought revenge. Sheppard, who was one of the less fortunate workers, followed the victim from Gosport towards his home near Titchfield. Then he went into an inn and asked to borrow a knife, on the pretext that he needed it to eat the provisions he had brought with him. The knife was found lodged in Harmsworth's throat, and when the murder enquiry began, the landlord identified it as the one he had lent Sheppard. When the latter was arrested, remains of blood and gore were discovered beneath his fingernails. He was taken into custody, and charged with the murder at the Winchester Assizes on 7 March. Although he pleaded not guilty, the evidence told a different story. It was not his family's first brush with the law, for he, along with his father and brother, had previously been charged with the manufacture of base coin, for which his brother had been convicted. After being convicted of wilful murder, Sheppard was hanged at Winchester gaol on 17 March.

9 MARCH   **1795**   Four prisoners were sentenced to death at Winchester Assizes: Joseph Weldon, for burglary; James Williams, for robbing Anna Arnold on the highway, 'and treating her at the same time very ill'; James Wright, for stealing sheep; and Joseph Cox, for violent assault on William Pellenger with intent to murder.

1777 James Aiken, alias James Hinde or James Hill, and known to posterity as 'Jack the Painter', was hanged. In December 1776, a mysterious fire began in the ropehouse at Portsmouth dockyard. Initially, the blaze was thought to be the result of an accident; then, about a month later, an incendiary device was discovered. Aiken had left the workforce at about the time of the fire. A few months earlier, he had visited several dockyards in the south of England, and found security surprisingly lacking. Being sympathetic towards the cause of American independence, he thought that doing something to cripple the British navy would be a good way of demonstrating solidarity with the rebels across the Atlantic. He laid a gunpowder trail, using hemp soaked in turpentine, and set light to it (having to go away and obtain some better matches, as the first ones were damp), then escaped. Once the device was found, suspicion fell on him, and a £50 reward was offered for his capture. He had left written instructions at his lodgings in Portsmouth, and when he was arrested for housebreaking at Odiham early next year, his similarity to the man wanted in connection with the dockyard fire was noted.

At his trial at Winchester, he was identified by the shopkeepers who had sold him the matches and turpentine. He confessed to the crime, was sentenced to death, and a mizzenmast from HMS *Arethusa* was erected as a gallows near the main gate of the dockyard. An hour after the execution, his body was cut down and taken across the harbour to Fort Blockhouse, where it was covered with a coat of tar and suspended for several years as a warning to others. It was later removed by some impecunious sailors who took it to an inn at Gosport to pay off a debt, and soon after that it was thought to have been buried at some unknown site on the coast nearby.

1941 Portsmouth suffered an air attack lasting about six hours, with German bombers coming over in waves and dropping bombs in sticks of six at a time. They were met by a heavy anti-aircraft barrage, and four of the enemy machines were destroyed. Two churches, a hotel used by local sailors and a club were all demolished in explosions, a synagogue was set on fire, and two post offices were damaged. Many private houses and business establishments suffered major damage, and one street was almost obliterated. A surface shelter was hit with two casualties, while three people were killed by a bomb which partly wrecked another shelter. A first-aid post was hit and five people slightly injured, while a car was thrown by the blast off the road and fell into a bomb crater. In several areas the civilian population were evacuated and taken to community centres. Altogether, 930 people were killed during Second World War bombing raids in Portsmouth, while 1,216 were injured.

1868 Stephen Locke, a brickmaker, was charged at Havant Petty Sessions with having made threats against John Hay, publican, at Rowland's Castle. Hay had been warned that Locke was coming to the inn with the intention of creating a disturbance, and had a policeman by the door ready to refuse him admittance. When Locke realised Hay's plan, he vowed to punch Hay in the head, offered to fight him for £5, and called him 'a big bee'. He was fined *2s 6d* and costs.

13 MARCH

1860   An inquest was held on the body of John Kempton at Alton. He and his son had been riding in a cart drawn by two horses, without reins or any other means of control, when the horses shied at some wheelbarrows in the road. In trying to get on the back of one of them, Kempton slipped: his trousers were caught in the shaft, and he hung with his head downwards for some time until, at last, the wheel passed over his head, and he fell dead into the road. The horses were stopped by another man, and a surgeon was sent for, but to no avail. A verdict of accidental death was returned.

14 MARCH

1849   Mary Kemp, of Ryde, was charged at the Petty Sessions in the town hall with assaulting Maria Gawn. She was fined 20s, but in default of payment was committed to a house of correction for twenty-one days.

15 MARCH

1875   A letter from actress and music-hall singer Jane Percy, who had appeared regularly in the camp and town of Aldershot for the last twenty years, appeared in a London newspaper. She described the Contagious Diseases Act as 'shameful and high-handed', and complained that the police were harassing her, placing her under surveillance and insisting she appeared for a medical examination at the hospital at twenty-four hours notice, merely because she had spent a great deal of time in the company of soldiers. Her husband had died of consumption about a year earlier and she had three small children to support, one of which, a daughter of 16, had just begun working on the stage with her. In a fury, she had terminated her engagement at Aldershot and left the town to go and stay with friends at Windsor, but as she could not find work elsewhere she returned a few days later, was promptly engaged by a music-hall agent for another season, and was again ordered to attend the hospital. When she refused, the music-hall proprietor, fearing the police might withdraw his licence, dismissed her.

On 28 March her body was found in the Basingstoke canal. A pantomime actor with whom she had worked in the past had seen her the previous evening, and later said she had seemed somewhat inebriated. At an inquest at the Military Hotel, Aldershot, on 30 March, the coroner said that she had probably intended to drown herself, but the jury failed to agree.

16 MARCH

Yarmouth, where the body of servant Florence Sebborn was washed ashore in March 1916.

1916   An inquest was held at Yarmouth on Florence Sebborn, a domestic servant whose body had been washed ashore on the coast. Her father had lost his life in saving her from drowning some years earlier, and her grandfather had died of burns after an accident at a firework display. A verdict of suicide was returned.

1922 The body of Lady Foster (76) was found in her nightdress at the bottom of the bath filled with water at her Southsea home. The cold water was still running, and the bathroom door was locked. Death was the result of shock from immersion in cold water, and it was at first suspected she might have deliberately killed herself, but at the inquest on 20 March it was suggested that she might have fainted and fallen in. Her friends said that she suffered from sleeplessness, but there were sufficient drugs found beside her bed to have enabled to take her life if she had intended to do so. An open verdict was recorded.

She was the widow of Sir T. Scott Foster, a Justice of the Peace and Mayor of Portsmouth, who had died in September 1918.

1738 Convicted of poisoning her mistress, servant girl Mary Grote/Groke (16) was tied to a hurdle and led in a procession behind a cart containing two men, John Boyd and James Warwick, who had also been sentenced to death for capital crimes, to Gallows Hill, outside Winchester. After the men had been hanged, she was chained to a large wooden stake. The executioner placed bundles of faggots around her and strangled her with a rope before setting light to them.

1885 An inquest was held on 19 March at Powell's Hotel, Shirley, on the bodies of John Cook (60), a former local publican and latterly shopkeeper, and his wife. The previous day a notice in his handwriting, saying that the premises would be closed for a few days, had been placed on the shutters. After the neighbours reported their suspicions that all was not well, the police forced an entrance, and discovered Mrs Cook's body in the passage, with a rope around her neck and a wound on her forehead. In an adjoining room, her husband was found slumped in a chair, with a rope around his neck and an empty laudanum bottle on the table. Mrs Cook, his second wife, was twenty years younger than him. She had suffered much from his violent temper, threats against her and abusive

Shirley, where John Cook killed his wife and himself in March 1885.

language. He had been jealous of a lodger, who had left some time since, with whom he suspected her of having an affair, and she had complained to her family.

Dr Caesar, who was called in after the bodies were discovered, believed that Mr Cook had secreted himself in the passage, and as his wife was going from the shop into the sitting room, where she was doing her sewing, he crept up behind her and struck her violently on the head, causing blood to bespatter the passage walls and her to fall down stunned. He strangled her, and then took their five-year-old son to a neighbour, Mrs Row, and asked her to take charge of him for a while as his mother was very ill. After placing a notice on the shop shutters, he wrote Mrs Row a letter appointing her executor of his will and guardian of the boy, wishing her to take possession of his house and property. The jury decided that his conduct had apparently been that of a sane person, and returned a verdict that he murdered his wife and took his own life while in a perfectly sound state of mind.

20 MARCH

1916 Mrs Peters, wife of a railway worker, of Suffolk Road, Eastney, killed her two sons, aged seven and five, and then herself. She had been suffering from depression for some time. A neighbour noticed a piece of paper with the words 'fetch a policeman' tied to the door of the house. She called a constable, who found the boys' bodies lying on a bed, and that of the mother on the floor beside them. A bloodstained carving knife was nearby.

21 MARCH

Netley Hospital, Southampton, where Captain Oldfield stayed for a while before taking his own life in March 1893.

1893 An inquest was held at Portsmouth on the body of Captain Edward Oldfield, late of the 2nd Battalion, 5th Fusiliers. He had been staying at Clarence House, Southsea, and had been in poor health for some time. His medical adviser went to see him in his room that morning but found the door locked. He forced his way in, and found the captain lying on the floor with his throat cut, and a bloodstained razor on the dressing table. Oldfield's father, Major-General Oldfield, said his son had enjoyed good health until about six years previously. While serving in India, he had a severe attack of typhoid fever, and was invalided home. Upon returning to India, he had an

even more severe attack, and for some time his life was despaired of. When sent home he was detained in an asylum at Calabar on his way back, and came home under restraint in a troopship. He remained at Netley Hospital for a time, and then went to a private asylum at Salisbury. A verdict of suicide while temporarily insane was returned.

22 MARCH

1861 William Smith and George Templeman broke into the house of Isaac Kenchington at Fordingbridge. The house had been left unoccupied for a short time in the middle of the day. When Mrs Kenchington returned, she found the house had been entered, and several articles taken away. Two sets of footprints were visible, and they were followed until the guilty men were found and overtaken, with the stolen articles on them. They appeared at Winchester

Assizes on 13 July, and were found guilty. A second charge against them was made. On the night of 19 March, Constable Smith was on duty in the London and Southampton turnpike road. The two men came from the Winchester direction in their regimental uniforms, and Smith demanded to see their passes. When they refused to show them, the constable threatened to arrest them: Smith knocked him down, while Templeman cut the staff from his hand, and then struck him on the head with a stick. Constable Smith, who was left covered with blood, said in court that he could positively identify them as his attackers, as he had seen their faces clearly in the moonlight. They admitted the crime, as well as the housebreaking, and were sentenced to six years' penal servitude.

1847 Charles Wolfe (20), a footman, was questioned in connection with an attempted murder. Elizabeth Ayling (18), a nurserymaid working for Mr William Thresher at Hamble, was in the nursery when Wolfe, who worked in the same house, entered the room with a mallet in his hand. She asked him what he was doing there; in reply, he left the room, returning with a razor. After striking her two violent blows on the head with the mallet, breaking the handle, he slashed her on the throat and in the neck with the razor while she lay prostrate, shouting, 'I'll Brown you!' (Brown was thought to be a rival admirer of hers.) Though she was semi-conscious, and had lost much blood, she struggled desperately with him and tried to grasp the razor from his hands, wounding her fingers severely in the process. At length she managed to escape from him and made her way to the kitchen, where the cook went and told the family. Wolfe was seized as he was about to cut his throat in front of a mirror. A messenger was sent to the police station and the footman was arrested.

    Miss Ayling's life had been despaired of for almost a week, but at length she recovered from her ordeal. A preliminary enquiry was held at the Red Lion Inn, Fareham, at which two other maidservants corroborated the evidence against Wolfe. He went on trial at Winchester Assizes in August and was sentenced to death, but this was commuted to transportation for life.

23 MARCH

1878 HMS *Eurydice*, a twenty-six-gun frigate launched in 1843, was caught in a heavy snowstorm off the Isle of Wight. She had sailed from Portsmouth on a three-month tour of the West Indies and Bermuda in November, and began her return voyage on 6 March under the command of Captain Marcus Hare. After an uneventful and fast passage across the Atlantic, she was seen eighteen days later by the coastguard at Bonchurch, near Ventnor, caught in a gale accompanied by a heavy snowstorm. She capsized and sank with only two survivors, and 378 people were either drowned or died from exposure in the freezing waters before they could be rescued.

24 MARCH

The unveiling of a monument to the officers and crew of HMS *Eurydice* in Shanklin Cemetery in June 1878. (*The Graphic*)

The sinking of HMS *Eurydice* in March 1878.

An inquiry established that her loss was due to bad weather conditions, and that no blame could be attached to the officers or crew, though it was felt that the ship was unsuitable as a training vessel as her design was known to lack stability.

25 MARCH   **1927** An inquest without a jury was held by Major Hugh Foster, coroner for North Hampshire, at the Cambridge Hospital, Aldershot. The deceased, Lieutenant-Colonel Douglas Hervey Talbot, commanding 17th/21st Lancers, had been found dead in his quarters on 23 March with a discharged Webley revolver lying at his feet and a bullet wound in his head. His brother John said that he had been very worried about the financial affairs of their father, who had recently died. Captain Charles Row said the wound was self-inflicted, and death was instantaneous.

26 MARCH   **1928** In the course of excavations made by Portsmouth City Council on Southsea Common, a complete human skeleton was unearthed about 2ft below the surface. There were marks of a deep wound in the unearthed skull, and the burial was thought to date from about a hundred years previously. Smuggling was common on the coast at that time, and the skeleton was presumably that of a man who paid for his activities with a sudden and violent death.

27 MARCH   **1881** A week of rioting in Basingstoke was brought to an end when the Mayor read the Riot Act. The unrest had begun on 20 March, when a gang charged the ranks of the Salvation Army as they led a procession through the town. The Mayor and police tried to restore order but failed, and several members of the public were injured in the fighting. The magistrates swore in a hundred special constables to help keep the peace, and on this day the Mayor proclaimed that everybody who did not go home there and then would be liable to penal servitude for life. The crowds quietly dispersed, and only one man, a drunk,

Basingstoke marketplace, close to the scene of a riot in March 1881.

was arrested. The *Pall Mall Gazette* reported scathingly on the 'roughs' having achieved their purpose of arranging a disturbance sufficient to afford a pretext for reading the Act and preventing the Salvation Army from their procession; 'and for the next hour Basingstoke was moved to fits of contemptuous laughter by watching the attempts of the Special Constables to clear the streets'.

28 MARCH   **1926** In a collision between two motorcyclists at the crossroads on the outskirts of Southampton, two riders and two pillion riders were seriously injured. One of the cyclists received a compound fracture of the thigh and wrist, and the other rider, Frederick Wakefield, of Chapel Terrace, Sholing, Southampton, was injured around the face and ribs. Reginald Dawson, a pillion rider, fractured the base of his skull, and the other rider, Mr Dedman, broke his left knee. The accident happened as a result of both riders trying to avoid a group of children playing in the middle of the road.

1644 Cheriton was the scene of a decisive defeat in the civil war for the royalist army under Sir Ralph Hopton. His troops (with another force under the Earl of Forth) planned to take control of New Alresford, to forestall an approaching contingent from the parliamentarian side. They occupied the town on 27 March.

Two days later, the latter, commanded by Sir William Waller, advanced and occupied Cheriton Wood. Hopton's forces attacked, and although the royalist army was smaller, they might have succeeded had it not been for one of his young, impetuous and poorly disciplined regimental commanders, Sir Henry Bard, who tried to take on the roundhead cavalry. His regiment was overwhelmed, and all his men were either killed or taken prisoner. After some bitter fighting, the royalist forces were driven back down what became known as the 'lane of disaster', which was said to be running with blood as a result. They sustained about 300 casualties, killed and wounded, while those on the other side numbered only about 60.

Left: The 'lane of disaster' at Cheriton, where royalist forces were pursued after a battle in March 1644.

Right: Sir Ralph Hopton, the defeated royalist commander at the battle of Cheriton in March 1644.

1830 The *Morning Chronicle* reported that a Commission of Lunacy had been executed at Gray's Inn Coffee House, to inquire into the state of mind of Richard Miles, aged about 33, of Manchester Street, London. In 1827 he had suffered some pain from and then went blind in one eye; after this, he threatened to kill himself.

On 28 October 1828, he went to Southampton and hired a boat to take him to Netley Abbey. During the voyage he cried bitterly, complaining that a gentleman at Ryde had insulted him. After arriving at Netley, he went ashore and stayed there a long time. When the boatman went into the abbey to find him, he found him leaning against a wall and crying. The man got him back into the boat, but on the journey back to Southampton he jumped on the seat of the boat and tried to throw himself into the water; the boatman stopped him. He made two similar attempts before they reached the mainland, and at the Southampton inn where he was staying he tried to cut his throat. To others, he said that people had accused him of contracting debts and swindling, that someone in the next house

The ruins of Netley Abbey, where the unfortunate Richard Miles paid a visit in March 1830.

had been murdered, that he had heard the cries of murder, and that the victim had been killed on account of his [Mr Miles's] confinement. He talked in a loud voice much of the day, apparently holding conversations with imaginary people.

At the time of his sister's wedding in August 1828 he had been judged perfectly sane, and the family made him one of her trustees. His behaviour deteriorated soon after that, particularly after his blind eye was removed: he had been fitted with a glass one, which was too large and caused him great irritation. He lived in dread of the complaint extending to his other eye, and then to his brain.

The jury, whom he denounced as 'a parcel of blackguards' when they visited him, and whose questions he refused to answer, found that he was insane, and that he had been in such a state since the time of his visit to Southampton.

31 MARCH   1885   An inquest was held on the body of James Alfred Henry Williams, aged six months, at the Windmill and Sawyer, Unicorn Road, Landport. He was the son of James Williams, of Trafalgar Street. The infant had slept with his mother on the night of 27 March, and next morning he was found dead by her side. Dr Ford gave evidence, and said that in his view the death must have been caused by convulsions, produced by meningitis. There was no sign of any marks on the child, and he did not think there was any chance of her having accidentally rolled over and suffocated the baby. The room in which the mother, three children and a woman named Clark slept in was very small, and the impure atmosphere, resulting from the lack of fresh air, might have been a contributory factor.

APRIL

Bordon High Street, where William Hall, manager of the local Lloyds Bank branch, was murdered in April 1924. (© *Nicola Sly*)

1 APRIL

1859 William Bramston, the driver of an omnibus which ran between Winchfield station and Odiham, had been missing for three days when his body was found hanging by a handkerchief from a tree in a shrubbery near the Beauclerc Arms, Winchfield. He had been discovered by the landlord, Edward Sturt. A groom, Daniel Draper, who had been a friend of the deceased for several years, said at the inquest on 4 April that Bramston had seemed very low-spirited as he had had notice to leave his situation, and it was his last day. As they were talking, the man who had been appointed to succeed him as driver was waiting for him to go and have his books examined by an official from the railway company. Several witnesses testified to his having recently been short of money, but said he 'did not seem of unsound mind', and spoke of him as a light drinker. The jury recorded a verdict that he took his own life, 'but we have not sufficient evidence before us to determine as [to] the state of his mind at the time'.

2 APRIL

1908 HMS *Tiger*, a 380-ton destroyer launched in 1900, was taking part in a home fleet exercise twenty miles south of the Isle of Wight, testing defences against torpedo boats. She crossed the bows of the cruiser HMS *Berwick*, and was sliced in half. Her bow section sank almost immediately, but the stern section stayed afloat long enough for most of the sixty-three crew to be rescued. The captain, Lieutenant Middleton, and twenty-seven members of the crew were drowned.

Left: HMS *Tiger*, destroyed with considerable loss of life of the Isle of Wight on 2 April 1908.

Right: A postcard printed to raise funds for the victims of HMS *Tiger*.

3 APRIL

1924 The body of William Hall, manager of the Bordon branch of Lloyds Bank, was found lying on the floor of the bank. He had been shot in the head and neck, and it was discovered that more than £1,000 had been stolen from the premises. Lance-Corporal Abraham Goldenberg, from the local army camp, came forward to tell police that he had been to the bank to cash a cheque and seen a red car outside in which there were two suspicious-looking men. However, Goldenberg was the one who was seen acting suspiciously a few days later! He was arrested, found to be in possession of £1,070 in banknotes, and proceeded to give two rambling, very different accounts of what had happened on the day Hall was killed.

At his trial at Winchester Assizes in June he was found guilty. Despite medical testimony arguing that he was insane, and a petition with over 100,000 signatures calling for a reprieve, Goldberg was executed on 30 July.

4 APRIL

1899 At the Quarter Sessions, Winchester Assizes, Blanche Caplin Gurnett (20) pleaded guilty to a charge of attempted suicide at Catherington by poisoning herself, and was bound over in her own recognisances to be of good behaviour and discharged. A similar judgement was made on George William Cutler, a fishmonger at Lymington who had tried to kill himself with a razor.

1881 Sophia Haskett and her daughter Alice were summoned for having 5 APRIL assaulted Lucy Woolf, a dairy woman from Stamshaw. Mrs Woolf alleged that over a period of several months she had been repeatedly harassed and verbally abused by the defendants. It came to a head on 30 March when she got out of her cart in Buckland Road to remonstrate with them. They struck her, and as she returned home they followed her, forced their way in through her front door and attacked her. In their defence, the Hasketts said Mrs Woolf, objecting to their bad language, hit out at one of them with a whip, and at the other with her hand. The magistrates expressed their belief that Mrs Woolf was the innocent party, and fined the Hacketts jointly 24s 6d.

1895 The body of a male child, wrapped up in a piece of newspaper, was picked 6 APRIL up on the shore at Southampton. The parcel was wet, and looked as if it had been thrown in the water overnight. Death was thought to have been the result of two severe fractures of the skull. Despite making enquiries, the police could not trace the parents, and at the inquest an open verdict was recorded.

1896 The body of Elsie Matthews (6) was found at Copnor on the outskirts 7 APRIL of Portsmouth. She had been strangled and her father, Philip Matthews, who worked as a coachman at Teignmouth, Devon, was arrested later that week at the Lamb Inn, Fareham. At the inquest, his wife Maria said that she had quarrelled with him about Charlotte Malony, the mistress with whom he had since eloped, and who had gone to the police with a full description of him after the murder enquiry was launched. Elsie was the daughter of his first wife, who had died in 1892 when the child was only eight months old. Maria insisted that she could not live with him any longer, and would not look after the child unless he promised to make ample provision for its maintenance. He drew up an agreement for their separation, which included the payment of 7s 6d a week for her to look after the girl. On 6 April he took Elsie away, saying that she would be well cared for in London. After being found guilty of murder, he was hanged by Billington on 21 June.

1953 An accident report on the fatal crash at Farnborough Air Show on 8 APRIL 6 September the previous year was released. The pilot, John Derry, the first British pilot to have exceeded the speed of sound in a British plane (four years earlier to the day), had just completed a low-level supersonic pass of the 120,000 spectators in a de Havilland DH.10 when he banked left to fly a wide circular turn. Heading towards the crowd, he started to pull the plane into a climb when the outer starboard wing, immediately followed by the outer port wing, broke off. The dramatic change in the centre of gravity of the aircraft resulted in both engines

The wreckage of the de Havilland DH.110 at Farnborough Air Show, for which a report was published in April 1953.

being torn from the airframe. One engine crashed harmlessly into some parked vehicles, but the other broke into two sections and ploughed into Observation Hill, injuring and killing several spectators. Derry, flight test observer Anthony Richards, and twenty-nine spectators were killed, and over sixty were injured. The report said that the combination of forces associated with both turning and straightening out had caused an instability in the airframe structure. Strict safety procedures were adopted as a result, and no member of the public has been killed at a British air show since.

9 APRIL

1886 The body of James Standley Parker (18) was found under a pile of straw in a field at Barton Hill, near Kings Worthy. His throat had been cut. Parker and Albert Brown (23) had been sailors on board the vessel *Nelly*, which had docked

Kings Worthy, close to where the body of James Parker was found in April 1886. (© *Nicola Sly*)

at Southampton the previous week, but were paid off and discharged as they were unsuited for the work. Police investigations soon led to Southampton Docks, and descriptions by other workers of Parker and Brown soon led them to the latter. Various items that had belonged to Parker were found in Brown's possession. He went on trial for murder at Winchester Assizes, was found guilty, and was hanged on 31 May.

10 APRIL

1912 The RMS *Titanic*, at that time the largest passenger steamship in the world, began her maiden voyage from the White Star line dock at Southampton, sailing for New York City. She stopped for additional passengers at Cherbourg and Cork, after which she had 2,240 people aboard. On the night of 14 April, she hit an iceberg and sank in less than three hours. 1,517 people died, leaving only 706 survivors and making it one of the worst peacetime disasters in maritime history. On 20 April, *Hampshire Chronicle* reported on the 'gloom in Southampton', where it was estimated that almost 1,000 local families had been directly affected.

One of the heroes of the occasion was Captain Sir Arthur Rostron, who ordered his ship, the Cunard liner RMS *Carpathia*, to sail nearly sixty miles through pack

Left: Memorial to the engineers who died on board the RMS *Titanic*, in East Park, Southampton.

Right: RMS *Titanic*, which sailed from Southampton in April 1912 and sank two days later.

ice to pick up survivors from the stricken ship, otherwise the casualties would have been much greater. He lived in Southampton for several years and was buried in West End, on the edge of the city. His gravestone commemorates his role in the rescue, and East Park has a monument erected in memory of the *Titanic*'s engineers, paid for by 'fellow engineers and friends throughout the world' and unveiled in April 1914.

1900 Mr W. Grammon, who had been City Surveyor at Winchester for twenty-four years, shot himself dead after a long illness. **11 APRIL**

1850 George Brooks, a farmer at Newport, fell from the stable loft, dislocated his neck and fractured his skull. An inquest next day at the Star Inn, Newport, recorded a verdict of accidental death. **12 APRIL**

1892 Nine young soldiers, all under 20 years old, were charged at the Hampshire Quarter Sessions with maliciously smashing plate-glass windows in Aldershot and Farnborough on various occasions during the preceding two months. They rambled drunkenly through the streets, wantonly breaking the tradesmen's windows with sticks as they passed. The chairman of the Bench warned them that such outrages had to be stopped, even if penal servitude had to be tried. Prior to February, property to the estimated value of £92 15s had been thus destroyed, and since then a further £170 10s had been lost. In reply to the chairman, an Aldershot police sergeant said he had not seen soldiers coming out drunk from the public houses so much as from the barrack canteens, and he reported it to the military police. Seven soldiers were sentenced to nine months' hard labour, and the other two to six months. **13 APRIL**

1885 The body of Richard Laishley (20), a waterman who lived at Havant Street, Portsea, was found drowned. He had been out the previous evening drinking with a few friends in the town, but he left them shortly after 11 p.m., saying he had to go and fetch his father's boat. Some minutes later he was seen coming in his boat from the Gosport direction, and as he came under the railway bridge a splash was heard, followed by a call of 'hurry up'. At about 4.15 a.m. he was discovered lying on the beach, with foam coming from the mouth. At the inquest at Portsmouth next day the coroner remarked on the unsatisfactory nature of the evidence, and though Dr Ford said that death was caused by drowning, the jury returned an open verdict. **14 APRIL**

1850 At Ryde Petty Sessions, Mr Hadley and Mr Bevis were convicted for drunken and disorderly conduct on the evening of 13 April. They were fined 5s each, and as they could not pay they were sent to the house of correction for fourteen days. **15 APRIL**

1863 William Goodwin (15), a naval cadet, fell down the hold of his training ship HMS *Boscowen* and was killed. At the inquest a verdict of accidental death was recorded. **16 APRIL**

17 APRIL   **1882**   Eliza Taifer, wife of Sergeant James Taifer, late of the Hampshire Militia, was brought up on a warrant, charged with assaulting and beating and using many threats towards him on 15 April, until he went in fear of his life. During the evening she was drunk and abusive, struck him with a pair of tongs, and threatened to kill him. On at least one previous occasion she had turned his daughter and her children out of doors, and in the past she been sent to prison in default of securities for similar violence and threats. Mr Taifer said he was willing to support her by a separate maintenance. She was ordered to find to sureties of £10 to keep the peace for two months, in default of which she would be imprisoned for that same period.

18 APRIL   **1890**   William Rouse, gamekeeper to Mr Currie, of Minley Manor, Blackwater, was shot during the evening while trying to apprehend a man who was acting suspiciously on Hawley Road. He had been with his young son and Mr Knight, a local gardener. The unknown man asked them the way to Reading. Knight told him it was about fifteen miles, and the man turned and went towards Hawley. When they followed him he started to run, and the three quickened their pace. Twice he fell, and the second time Rouse fell over on top of him. Young Rouse and Knight saw a revolver flash in the darkness, came to William Rouse's assistance, and found the gamekeeper had been shot. With assistance they carried him to the Red Lion Inn, but he died from his wounds about an hour later.

Meanwhile, Knight had followed the man, but retreated when the killer pointed his revolver at him, saying angrily, 'I'll serve you the same.' The gunman went on to the Royal Swan Inn, where he told the landlord he had been assaulted by three men, and thought he had shot one of them. Meanwhile, Knight called a policeman, Constable Reynolds, and they eventually captured the man with the gun, one Samuel Milner (31), a surgeon. He offered a desperate resistance before he was taken to the room where Rouse lay dying, and as he drew his last breath the latter pointed at his assailant and said weakly, 'that's him'. Milner appeared very upset, saying, 'I am very sorry, what a shocking thing to take the life of an innocent man.'

He appeared at Winchester Assizes on 29 July, where the jury agreed with the counsel for the defence that Milner was 'the assailed and not the assailant', and that he shot Rouse but in self defence. He was found not guilty, and the judge ordered that he should be detained for a few hours and then discharged from the gaol.

19 APRIL   **1899**   Charles Maidment (22), a labourer, murdered his former fiancée Dorcas Houghton at Swanwick. She had broken off their engagement, and arranged a meeting to return his gifts. He tried to persuade her to reconsider and go out with him again, but she refused. They went for a walk along Swanwick Lane, where he drew a revolver and shot her dead. He then went to Fareham Police Station and gave himself up, handing them the revolver, of which five of the six chambers were still loaded. At his trial at Winchester Assizes on 27 June, he and his defence pleaded insanity, but he was found guilty and hanged on 18 July.

Main: An artist's impression of the murder of Miss Houghton at Swanwick in April 1899. *(Illustrated Police News)*

Insets: Charles Maidment and Dorcas Houghton, whose broken engagement ended in her murder and his execution in 1899. *(Hampshire Telegraph & Sussex Chronicle)*

1872 An inquest was held at the Railway Hotel, Portswood, on the body of Charles Smith, a labourer, buried alive the previous afternoon in a sandpit at Portswood Park. He and a fellow labourer had been drawing sand up from the 24ft deep pit in buckets when the ground suddenly gave way and he fell down. His body was recovered later that evening, cold and long since dead. At the hearing ,the men's employer, Mr Conway, was censured for having promised to find timber to shore up the pit, according to witnesses, though he denied having done anything of the kind as he had no timber to spare. Nevertheless, a verdict of accidental death was recorded.

20 APRIL

Portswood Road, close to the sandpit where Charles Smith was accidentally buried alive in April 1872.

1885 Isaac Paul and William Cooper, both aged 12, were charged at Portsmouth Police Court with stealing a piece of mutton, valued at 6d, the property of Charles George Withers, a butcher in Fratton Street. In the evening they were seen loitering near the shop by Detective Parrett, who saw them go to a scraper fixed to the front of a house nearby and take the meat from it. Cooper placed the stolen meat under his coat, and both were walking away when the policeman stopped them. The meat was identified by Withers, and the boys were led to the police station. On the way, Cooper dropped a stick, to which was affixed

21 APRIL

a nail, which had evidently been used in removing the meat from the shop board. Mr Silk, the Chief School Attendance Officer, said that both boys were known to be of bad character, and were beyond the control of their parents. They had been before the court for various similar petty offences, and this time they were sentenced to fourteen days' hard labour and then five years in a reformatory.

22 APRIL   **1919**   Five airmen, members of the Royal Air Force, were burned to death in an accident which befell a Handley Page machine at Weyhill Aerodrome, about two miles from Andover. The aeroplane had taken off soon after 2.30 a.m. on a morning of bright moonlight with very little breeze, and conditions were ideal. After the signal was given to start, the machine did not take off quickly enough. She turned in a southerly direction, but failed to clear the roof of one of the permanent dormitories on one side of the aerodrome. The under-carriage was carried away by the force of the impact, and a hole was smashed in the side of the wall and the roof of the sleeping hut. The machine fell to the ground with a crash, the petrol in the tank immediately caught fire, and the whole aeroplane was enveloped in flames. The aerodrome staff were soon on the spot, but could not help the airmen, who were pinned beneath the wreckage, because of the intense heat of the flaming petrol in the tank. Two of the crew managed to fall partially clear of the machine and were either dragged or crawled out of further danger, but they were badly injured and had to be taken to Tidworth Military Hospital.

23 APRIL   **1867**   Shortly before the arrival of the 4.10 p.m. train from Southampton to Basingstoke, a telegraph message was received by the station officials to detain a man, apparently a foreigner, until a gentleman employed in the Southampton government office could reach Basingstoke. Although the mysterious foreigner was found, he was not placed under arrest, and was allowed to walk around the platform. About half an hour later, his body was discovered lying at the back of a coalstack adjoining the terminus of the Great Western Railway, surrounded by a pool of blood. He was bleeding from a cut across his throat, presumably self-inflicted, and he died shortly afterwards. He had arrived at Southampton from France, *en route* to Liverpool. There was a large sum of money in his possession, and while he was exchanging some for American currency at Southampton an irregularity, probably relating to fraud or forgery, had been detected. Because of this a telegraph was despatched requesting his apprehension.

24 APRIL   **1951**   An eleven-day trial at Winchester Assizes of eight persons charged with conspiring to break and enter Barclays Bank, Waterlooville, and steal from safes, was concluded. Henry Bryan, a bookmaker from Islington, described by Mr Justice Byrne as the brains of the conspiracy, was sentenced to ten years' imprisonment and ordered to pay £2,000 towards the prosecution costs. Four others were given lesser custodial sentences, one was placed on probation for three years, and the other two were discharged. The judge said that the police and officers of the Post Office Investigation department involved were all worthy of the highest commendation in 'bringing a very dangerous gang of criminals to justice'.

1660 Richard Major died at his home, Hursley Park, Merdon. A wealthy landowner, he had been an ardent supporter of Parliament during the Civil War, and his daughter Dorothy married Oliver Cromwell's son Richard in 1649. In 1653, Major represented Southampton in Parliament, and in the following year he was elected for Hampshire. After Cromwell died and Richard resigned from the protectorship, Major retired from public life. When it became apparent that the monarchy was going to be restored, he feared he would be charged with treason as a leading adherent of the old regime and his sudden death led to rumours, admittedly unsubstantiated, that he had committed suicide. He was buried in the chancel of Hursley Church on 30 April.

1888 George Augustus Early, aged about 19, who had completed his allotted period of separate confinement at Winchester Gaol, was removed to a penal establishment at Chatham. On 13 April 1887 he had shot his sweetheart Isabella Ann Fleming (20) at her home at St Mary's Road, Southampton. The young couple had been keeping company for four years and were engaged ,despite the disapproval of her parents, who thought he was of 'unsettled habits'. Both young people were alone in the kitchen that afternoon, when Mrs Fleming heard two pistol shots, and a scream of 'Oh, mother, he has shot me!' She ran in to find her daughter leaning against the wall, shot in the right breast, while Early was lying on the floor bleeding from a wound in his mouth. A pistol lay nearby. The girl died about five minutes later. When the doctor arrived, her distracted mother said, 'Save my daughter, and let that villain go; I hope he will die!' He was removed to the infirmary, and was still convalescent when he appeared before the Southampton Borough Police Court on 20 May 1887.

At his trial, at Winchester on 30 July, it was suggested that Early was drunk at the time of the attack, and had shot her to prevent anybody else from marrying her. His defence counsel, Mr Giles, said that the prisoner had tried to take his own life, and when Miss Fleming tried to prevent him, the weapon accidentally exploded. When the judge pointed out that Early had never said it was an accident, Giles said that his solicitor had advised the prisoner's solicitor to say nothing. 'Then all I can say is that more pernicious advice was never given,' replied the judge, 'and his solicitor, who is sitting in the background, ought to be ashamed of himself for ever.' Early was sentenced to death, but this was commuted to life imprisonment, first at Winchester, then Chatham, then Parkhurst. In August 1900, he was released on the recommendation of the Home Secretary.

1894 William Atkinson (48), a retired naval commander, was found dead in his lodgings at Penny Street, Portsmouth. At the inquest at Portsmouth Town Hall on 1 May, Richard Williams, of the same address, said he had known Atkinson for about five years and knew he was an alcoholic. On 26 April, he had returned to the premises very drunk, and gone straight up to his room. Williams checked regularly on him up to about 1.30 a.m. and found him apparently asleep. At 10 a.m. he found him lying dead on the floor. One of the jurors suggested that the dead man had been suffering from heart disease, and might have fallen during an epileptic fit. Dr Morley, who conducted the post-mortem, said he had suffocated after falling on his face and flattening his nose to the level of his cheek bones. Mrs Pannell, at whose house he had lodged for several months previously, said he very rarely came home sober, and she had never known him have an epileptic fit. The jury gave a verdict that he had been accidentally suffocated by falling on his face while in a state of drunkenness.

28 APRIL   **1820**   James Ings, one of the Cato Street conspirators, was executed. He was born in Portsea and had run a butcher's shop until it failed in 1819 and he moved to London. Coming into contact with several radicals who, like him, had been horrified by the Peterloo massacre, he joined the conspirators (who intended to kill a group of government ministers going to dine together at a

London house in February 1820). The police had been forewarned, the plot failed, and the would-be assassins were arrested. Eleven were charged, one of these agreed to give evidence against the others in court, and five were sentenced to transportation for life. Ings was one of the remaining five hanged at Newgate Gaol.

The Cato Street conspirators, including Portsea-born James Ings, were executed at Newgate in April 1820.

29 APRIL   **1913**   An inquest was held on the body of Lieutenant L.C. Rogers-Harrison, 2nd Royal Warwickshire Regiment, who was killed in an aeroplane accident at Farnborough. He was piloting a biplane which, according to witnesses, 'burst in the air' at a height of 400ft and pitched downwards, turning over as it fell into a field a few hundred yards north of the aeroplane factory. Assistance arrived immediately, but Harrison was already dead.

30 APRIL   **1885**   James Morey (46), a baker at Southsea, was found dead. An inquest was held on 1 May at the Cobden Arms, Arundel Street, Portsmouth. He had lived with his sister Charlotte at Landport, and suffered from rheumatism for some years. On the evening of 29 April he returned from work, and complained of pain in his legs. After having tea, he went to bed about 11 p.m. feeling very unwell; he slept in a back parlour downstairs. At 8.15 a.m. the next day, Charlotte called him, and when he did not answer she entered the parlour and found him lying dead on the sofa. She summoned Dr John Palmer, who conducted a post-mortem: this found that the liver was enlarged and the kidneys diseased. The doctor thought death was caused by corrosive matter in the stomach. In a glass beside the body was found traces of binoxalate of potash, known as essential salts of lemon or salts of sorrel; ½ oz in the stomach would have been sufficient to cause death. The circumstances did not point to suicide, and there was no evidence to show how the deceased became possessed of the poison. The coroner asked the jury to return a verdict that he died from taking poison, but there was insufficient evidence to enable the jury to decide how or why poison was administered.

MAY

A typical coroner's inquest of the late Victorian era; sudden deaths and tragic accidents, such as the immolation of 2 year-old Sarah Emily Harding on 7 May, would have been discussed in a room like this one.

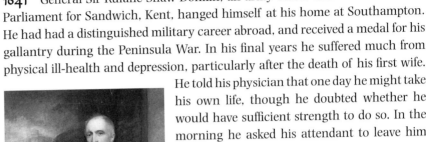

1 MAY

1841 General Sir Rufane Shaw Donkin, an army officer and later Member of Parliament for Sandwich, Kent, hanged himself at his home at Southampton. He had had a distinguished military career abroad, and received a medal for his gallantry during the Peninsula War. In his final years he suffered much from physical ill-health and depression, particularly after the death of his first wife.

Sir Rufane Donkin, who hanged himself at his Southampton home in May 1841.

He told his physician that one day he might take his own life, though he doubted whether he would have sufficient strength to do so. In the morning he asked his attendant to leave him undisturbed for a while, as he felt very tired. He then locked the door. When his servant could not get any answer, he called the doctor. They had to force an entry by taking a ladder round to the window, and on entering the room they found the general's body suspended by a handkerchief from the rail at the foot of the bedstead. At the inquest, a verdict of 'temporary insanity' was recorded.

2 MAY

1809 Mr Blanchard of Gosport had made a bet of a hundred guineas that his mare would trot from the town to three miles beyond Chichester, and back again, in six hours, a distance of sixty miles. He undertook the ride, but as they returned, the exhausted animal collapsed at Fareham and died.

3 MAY

1875 In the morning Mr Church at Everton near Lymington noticed that the door of his neighbour, George Haskell, had the key on the outside. He went inside the house, and was horrified to see Haskell hanging by the neck from a ledge over the front of the staircase. Instead of cutting him down at once, Church went in search of other members of Haskell's family. They did not want to touch the body either when they arrived, so they sent for a policeman. He cut it down, an hour and a quarter after Haskell had made the discovery. Though limp, the body was warm. It was regretted that Church had not done so himself at first, as he might have saved the man's life. Haskell, aged 53, had been seen talking to a neighbour the previous evening, and seemed in good spirits. Nevertheless, he had recently lost his job, and was said to have had family troubles.

4 MAY

1874 Thomas Clowser, a builder and estate agent at Hampstead, received a letter from William Etherington, a chemist, in which he stated that he had witnessed conduct on the part of Clowser's son and a servant girl which he believed would probably lead to a similar tragedy to that of a recent case at Eltham, in which a soldier had murdered a young girl the previous year. The conduct alleged was said to have been seen taking place in a room above the drawing room, and the writer said that, as he wrote for the press, and belonged to 'a certain society', he should feel bound to make the matter public. However, if Mr Clowser would satisfy him for his trouble, he would say no more about it. Clowser replied to the letter, and received a reply from Etherington, who had since gone to Winchester, saying that if he (Clowser) would send him a cheque for £5, no further reference would be made to the matter. A postal order for 20s was sent to him, and when he presented it at the Winchester post office he was apprehended by a detective who had been watching him. He was tried at the Central Criminal Court for sending threatening letters 'under very peculiar circumstances', found guilty, and sentenced to twelve months' imprisonment.

1831 Admiral Sir J.S. Yorke, Captain Matthew Bradby, Captain Thomas Young, and seaman John Chandler were returning from Spithead on the 14-ton yacht *Catherine*, near Browndown Point, between Portsmouth and Hamble. At about 4 p.m. a sudden squall took the vessel, which immediately went down stern foremost. The accident was seen by a fisherman about half a mile off, and he went to their assistance at once. He first came to Chandler, who had been in the water about five minutes, but was speechless and exhausted. The next ten minutes were occupied in well-meant but unsuccessful attempts to save his life. The other three men 'floated without attention, being completely enveloped in their cloaks and great coats, which so encumbered and concealed their bodies, as to be mistaken for empty garments'. By the time the fisherman discovered otherwise, they were dead. The body of Yorke had floated further down and was picked up by another boat. **5 MAY**

1882 Robert Gibbs, of Westminster Place, Newport, assaulted his wife Priscilla at their home while he was drunk. He came home in the evening, knocked on the door and asked her if he could come in. She told him he could, as long as he kept quiet. He came in, put some groceries on the table, hung his coat up, and then began swearing at her and her daughter. She reminded him that he had promised to be quiet, so he got up, grabbed her by the throat, tried to strangle her, and pulled some of her hair out. Her daughter, also called Priscilla, tried to come to her rescue, but he turned on her and pulled some of her hair out as well. Her son went to fetch Mr Greenham, a neighbour, but as he was not at home Mrs Greenham came instead. She tried to release Mrs Gibbs from her husband's grasp, but as she failed she went out for further assistance. Mr Gibbs followed Mrs Greenham out, and Mrs Gibbs bolted the door behind them. **6 MAY**

When the case came to court on 8 May, Mrs Gibbs said that they had been married for twenty-six years. She suffered from a bad leg, the result of erysipelas, and one day, about three weeks ago, when she was resting it on a chair, he spitefully sat down on it and had to be pulled off by a neighbour. Among those giving corroborative evidence as to his drunkenness, violence and cruelty to his wife were her daughter, Mrs Greenham, and Constable Spanner. Gibbs was sentenced to three months' imprisonment with hard labour, and a separation order was granted to his wife, with an allowance of 8s per week to support her and her family.

Newport, where a drunken Robert Gibbs assaulted his wife in May 1882.

7 MAY

1881 An inquest was held on the body of Sarah Emily Harding (2) at the East Hants Cricket Ground Club House, Southsea. Her mother Emily said that on the morning of 20 March she was in the kitchen of their Southsea house with Sarah and her four other children. A fire was burning in the grate, and she had just put some sticks on to make the fire burn up when she was distracted by somebody knocking on the door, and went to talk to her caller for about five minutes. She then heard the children screaming, and found Sarah lying on the floor with her nightdress on fire. She wrapped the skirt of her dress around her, put out the flames, and went to call for assistance. Sarah's chest, stomach and right arm were badly burned. A surgeon came to attend to her, but, although the wounds showed signs of healing, she had severe convulsions on 5 May, and died twenty-four hours later. Although the fire was surrounded by a guard more than 2ft high, one of the deceased's sisters, aged five, said she had taken a lighted stick from the fire to play with. A verdict of accidental death was returned.

8 MAY

1920 Frederick Messenger (17) died in the kitchen at the family farm, Lower Wield. His mother Annie told his brother Norman on his arrival home that Fred, who was severely disabled, had had a fit and burst a blood vessel. When the doctor and a policeman arrived to find him lying in a pool of blood, they realised that he had been shot in the head. A shotgun found hanging on a beam in the kitchen smelt strongly of gunpowder, suggesting it had been fired very recently. An inquest was opened on 11 May and adjourned, and on 14 May, Annie Messenger and another son, Philip Westbrook, the deceased's half-brother, were arrested and charged with feloniously killing him. The inquest was resumed on 27 May, and after suicide was ruled out on the grounds that Fred was too disabled to load and fire the weapon himself, a verdict of murder by person or persons unknown was returned.

Lower Wield, where Frederick Messenger was shot dead in May 1920.

Mrs Messenger and Philip Westbrook went on trial on 7 July at Winchester Assizes, but as it opened, Ernest Charles, counsel for the prosecution, announced that a confession had been received, and he would not be offering any evidence to the court. A statement had been made by Fred's 11-year-old brother Reginald, saying he had taken the gun down to clean and accidentally shot his brother. He ran away as he was so frightened, and only plucked up the courage to tell his uncle several weeks later. Although his mother and half-brother walked free from court, speculation remained that his confession was a shrewd way of securing their freedom, and that they had staged the 'accident' in order to remove the burden of caring for a sick relative from their lives. The policeman who examined the body had been astonished at Mrs Messenger's calm demeanour, even to the point of laying the kitchen table and sitting down for their next meal while her son's body lay on the floor.

1876   Peter Dykstria, a sergeant serving in the Dutch army, had left Niew   9 MAY
Diep with his detachment on board *König des Nederlands*, bound for Batavia. While sailing for England, he told his lieutenant that he would not live long. On 14 May. he was seen attempting to throw himself overboard. Every effort was made to save him, but when his body was brought back on deck he was dead. An inquest at Southampton returned a verdict of suicide.

1691 'Old Mobb'   10 MAY
Thomas Sympson, known as 'Old Mobb', was born in Romsey around 1650. He was well known as a highwayman who usually dressed as a woman while frequenting the roads of southern England and the West Country, tending to rob wealthy aristocrats. As with most others of his profession, his luck eventually ran out and he was hanged at Tyburn in May 1691.

A highwayman of the late sixteenth or early seventeenth century.

11 MAY

1890 Mr Clark, landlord of the Foresters Arms, West Street, Southampton, had an altercation with one of his customers, a tramp visiting the town, just before closing time in the afternoon, and asked him to leave. The man refused, and there was a struggle between them. Mr Clark suddenly fell down and died.

12 MAY

1899 Two suicides, both independent cases, were reported to have taken place at Southsea.

At about 5.30 a.m., Charlotte Over (39) was found hanged at the family home at Telephone Road. The grim discovery was made by her brother George when he got up to go to work. She was to have been married on 24 May, and over the previous few weeks she had seemed very depressed. That same afternoon, Robert Coleman (37), a hawker who lived at Silver Street and who had been prevented from attending to his business for some time by severe asthma, cut his throat with a small cheese knife. A doctor was sent for and hurried to the house, but Coleman was dead within a few minutes.

13 MAY

1899 Edward Marks, a tobacconist at Lake Road, Landport, had a narrow escape with his wife and child when a fire in their shop broke out during the night. It was discovered shortly before 3 a.m., and it took the fire services over an hour to extinguish the blaze. The family, sleeping upstairs, were awakened by the smoke, but were unable to come down the stairs because of smoke and flames. They managed to escape by sliding down a rope at the back of the shop, the rope being attached to a windowsill with a large nail. By morning it was seen that the shop and back living rooms were completely burnt out, and the bedrooms were extensively damaged.

14 MAY

1874 Henry Thomas had an altercation with Alfred Samphire, a labourer, at Gosport. The latter took the case to the police, and Thomas appeared at Gosport Police court on 19 May. Samphire alleged that Thomas had 'rambled against him' and knocked him down. He was not charged, but the Bench warned both men to behave better in future.

15 MAY

1852 During the night an intruder broke into Mr Meeres's farm, Golden Ball Street, Petersfield, and poisoned four valuable pigs. Two were found dead next morning, but the other two recovered. When the stomachs of the dead ones were opened, it was discovered that pieces of hemlock had been chopped up into very small pieces and mixed with their ordinary food.

16 MAY

1882 George Merritt (26), a labourer from Bramdean Common, was killed by injuries sustained while working on a traction engine near the Common. He, Henry Vince, and John Fisher had charge of an engine on the high road from Ropley to Alresford on the morning of 12 May, and as they drew near the Common they stopped to enter a narrow lane. The steam was turned off, and without waiting to check whether the mechanism had completely stopped, Merritt went to take out the coupling irons so they could check that they were in good working order. The engine ran backwards towards him and hit him in the right thigh. He was taken to the Royal Hants County Hospital, but died of his injuries four days later.

1926 Sergeant Ralph Hawkins, a pilot from Blackpool, and Leading
Aircraftsman Sidney Cox of Bristol were killed in the afternoon when their
aeroplane crashed. The men were attached to No. 12 (Bombing) Squadron,
stationed at Andover, and were taking part with eight other machines in
formation practice at Abbotts Inn. They were flying a Faerie Fawn, and were
about to return to the aerodrome when it fell from a height of about 1,000ft,
and crashed in a field 60yds away. A witness who had been watching the
practice said that the plane looked like it had developed some trouble, 'got into a
spin, which was followed by a bang louder than that of a motor-car backfiring,
and then dropped like a stone'.

1898 George Henry Pottle (32), a bricklayer of Southsea, was charged at
Portsmouth Police Court on a warrant with neglecting his five children, aged
between six and twelve years. Mr G. Hall King, prosecuting on behalf of the
National Society for the Prevention of Cruelty to Children, said that in January
Pottle had been brought up on a similar charge – but as he alleged the neglect
was due to the fact that he could not get work, and promised to take them and go
into the Union, the magistrates gave him another chance. However, he did not
go into the Union, but returned to his father's house. Making no effort to find
work, he went out drinking, and continued to neglect the children. His wife was
so angry that she walked out on him, but left him in charge of the youngsters
who, because of the lack of care given to them, were only one-third of what
should have been their normal weight at their ages. Their grandfather, Edward
Pottle, also a bricklayer, said he did not have the heart to turn them out, though
he had nearly been forced into the workhouse in the effort to maintain them as
he had had to pawn most of his possessions. His son, he went on, knew his trade
well and was capable of earning £1 17s a week if he really wanted to. He drank
what little he did earn, and during the last six weeks had only contributed 15s
6d for supporting the children. His mother corroborated this evidence, saying
she and her husband had done their best for the children, but could not get
enough food for them.

George Pottle pleaded guilty and asked the magistrates to give him another
chance, but he was told that, in spite of being warned, he had persistently
neglected his family and gone about drinking with 'bad companions'. A sentence
of three months' imprisonment with hard labour was handed down, but a
separate charge against the prisoner for assaulting his mother was not proceeded
with.

1861 Alicia Regan, a single woman, was drinking in the saloon of the White
Hart, Gosport, during the evening. She had only been there a few minutes when
James Crow, another customer, was seen to take a piece of paper and light it at
the gas jet. He then set her clothes on fire. The landlord put the flames out and
took Crow into custody. Apart from being badly shocked, she was apparently
unharmed. When he appeared at Winchester Assizes on 13 July, the prisoner
could offer no explanation for his behaviour. In summing up the case, Mr Justice
Byles said that in all his experience he had never known such a case, and he
thought the statute law 'did not meet the case of setting fire to the inflammable

The White Hart Inn, Gosport, where Alicia Regan was attacked in May 1861. (© *Diane Webb*, 2010)

dresses now worn by one-half of the species'. Although no actual bodily harm had been done, the offence amounted to a common assault at common law. After the jury had found Crow guilty, the judge told him that had the fire not providentially been put out at once, and if death had ensued, he would have been tried for murder. He was sentenced to six months' imprisonment.

20 MAY

1880   According to a written statement made by his 19-year-old wife Eveline, Theodore Lane, an actor of Southsea, was shot dead on this day and his body thrown into the sea. She was arrested a few days later at Havant on a charge of larceny, and then confessed to being an accessory to her husband's killing. When charged at Portsmouth Police Court on 1 June, she fell down in the dock, apparently in a fit. A doctor and a constable agreed that she was 'shamming'; she had been in custody all night and was perfectly sober. According to the statement, she said that she and her husband had spent the afternoon at Portsmouth, and then went to Southsea Common, where they met another man. He had a bottle of brandy with him, and poured Theodore some, making him very drunk.

Royal Naval Barracks, Portsmouth, c. 1900. Eveline Lane claimed that she was going to run away with an artilleryman from the barracks, but the story was found to be false.

At about 10.45 p.m. the two men had had a quarrel – whereupon the man produced a revolver, shot Theodore and threw him into the sea. After seeing this happen, she left the scene, having promised to meet the other man at a later date. He was an artilleryman, quartered in Gun Wharf Barracks, Portsmouth, and had promised to desert the army and take her away. Her mother, she said, knew nothing of her being married, though the wedding had taken place two years ago. In court she confirmed that the statement was true, and then asked whether she would be hanged.

She was remanded in custody and brought before the magistrates a second time on 3 June. It was then shown that her story was a complete fabrication, and she was discharged. Immediately afterwards, she was apprehended by the Isle of Wight police on a charge of felony.

1802 Three gentlemen were returning in a post-chaise from Somerset to Gosport. The driver was not paying sufficient attention to the way in front of him, and near Titchfield they overturned and were thrown into the road. One broke his right arm, and the other two were badly bruised, but all three made a good recovery within several days. 21 MAY

1919 Thomas Carney (71), of Aldershot, made three attempts to take his own life by throwing himself under a bus, a car and a steam lorry in High Street. When apprehended, he said he was tired of life. He was committed for trial at Winchester Assizes. 22 MAY

Aldershot High Street in around 1910, where Thomas Carney made three unsuccessful attempts to commit suicide in May 1919.

1885 A Portsmouth schoolboy, Masters, died after being hit by one of his fellow pupils. On 13 May, he and John Broad were on their way home from school, when Masters insulted Broad. The latter hit him in the stomach, causing him severe pain. A doctor was called to attend to Masters at home: he found him in bed, screaming in agony. After Masters died, a post-mortem examination was conducted, and it was found that the abdomen was much discoloured, with internal evidence of violence. The cause of death was due to exhaustion 'provoked by excessive violence', resulting in peritonitis. A blow would have certainly produced this condition, especially if the recipient was struck unawares. In summing up, the coroner pointed out that as Broad was under seven years of age, he was not legally responsible for his actions and could not be sent for trial on a charge of felony. By his direction, the jury found a verdict to the effect that the deceased died from peritonitis resulting from the blow. 23 MAY

1934 Mrs Gwynedd Hyacinth Kennard (31) died from morphia poisoning at the house of Dr Henry Stanley, in Fairfield Terrace, Havant. She had moved in with him in October 1933 after leaving her husband, whom she claimed was ill-treating her. Dr Stanley had never treated her as a patient, though at the inquest at Portsmouth on 1 June he said he was aware that she was drinking heavily and had also taken drugs. Her father, Admiral John Nicholas, told the court that he and his wife had offered to take Kennard back into their home. He said he thought she had taken her life while in a state of distraction because Dr Stanley 24 MAY had alleged that she had associated on one occasion with another man, and said 'he would bring that up to her every day of his life'. The coroner for South Hampshire, Leonard Warner, said that the circumstances surrounding the life of Mrs Kennard, her husband, and Dr Stanley were so unusual that he could not avoid going into the whole question to make certain that no blame should be attached to anyone but the deceased for her death. Satisfied that there was no criminal responsibility on the part of anyone else, he recorded a verdict of 'suicide while of unsound mind'.

25 MAY   1881   Caroline Emma Richardson (10) was brought before the Court by Mr Ford, superintendent of the School Board, after having been found that morning in a destitute condition in Union Street, Portsea. Her mother lived in Southampton Row with six other prostitutes, and had neglected her for some time. An order was made that she should be detained at the local workhouse for a week, while enquiries could be made as to her parochial settlement.

26 MAY   1919   An accident occurred at Farnborough aerodrome during a first trial flight of a triplane designed by Mr Tarrant, a building contractor of Weybridge, assisted by Captain P.T. Rawlings, DFC, late of the Royal Naval Air Service, who had taken up an appointment as general manager of the aeroplane department. The machine, which, when loaded, weighed 22 tons and stood 75ft high, had a wingspan of 140ft. It appeared to be travelling and turning satisfactorily at first, running on its landing wheels with an occasional lift; but once the upper engines were brought into play, the machine pitched bodily forward and almost buried its

front and main parts in the ground, smashing and grinding its way about 6ft into the soil. A first-aid motor ambulance and fire-fighting apparatus, kept ready at the factory, were on the spot within seconds of the accident, and the crew were quickly rescued from the wreck. Everyone involved had been injured: Rawlings and Captain F.G. Dunn, who had co-piloted the plane between them, were the most seriously hurt of all. They were admitted to the Cambridge Hospital, but Rawlings died an hour later and Dunn survived for two days with a fractured skull and spine, never regaining consciousness before his death on 28 May.

Aldershot Cambridge Military Hospital, where the injured were admitted after an air accident at Farnborough in May 1919.

27 MAY   1884   Tom Walker (21), of Chalton Park Terrace, Portsmouth, was charged at the police court with attempting suicide. On 24 May he had left his job, where he had been employed for the last two years, with a good character, and went home to the back of his house with a box of matches. His mother thought he seemed rather excited, and heard a noise at the back of the house. When she went to check, she found that he had fastened a rope to one of the rafters of the wash house. She called a male neighbour for help, and he found the prisoner standing on a chair with a rope around his neck. He cut the rope, and Walker got off the chair, telling the man to leave him alone. The police were informed, and he was

arrested. He told his mother that he had lost some money, and it was thought he had been betting. In court he said he had acted on impulse, was very sorry for what he had done, and promised not to do so again. He was remanded in gaol for seven days.

1843   James Knight (45), a travelling dealer in tea and other goods, had travelled in a gig from Salisbury to Romsey earlier in the week, and stayed at the Angel Inn for two days. After being pressed for payment, he left and slept at Bishop Blaise Inn nearby. On this day, at about 10 a.m. the landlady went up to his room and found Knight's body suspended by his braces from the bedpost. Papers were found in his pocket, including two cards with notes written to friends bidding them farewell and giving directions for his funeral. At the inquest a verdict of suicide was recorded, and his body was interred in the churchyard at Romsey by night without any Christian burial rites.   28 MAY

1888   An altercation between Emanuel Emanuel and Morris Goodstone, two shopkeepers from Portsea, led to a charge of assault at Portsmouth Police Court on 8 June. Goodstone said he had known Emanuel for some years, although neither had ever spoken to the other before. Between 11 a.m. and midday, Goodstone was standing by his shop when Emanuel beckoned him into his premises, took him by the shoulder, told him he was 'a bloody impostor' imposing upon poor people, and spat in his face. Goodstone, he declared, pretended to be poor but could not be, as he had recently received between £70 and £80 from a fire insurance company. Three witnesses, also local traders, claimed to have witnessed the physical and verbal attack that day.   29 MAY
   Emanuel claimed in his defence that it was 'one of the most infamous concoctions against a respectable citizen' who had been born in the borough and had lived his whole life there that could possibly be made. He complained that Goodstone had committed a flagrant violation of the law by obstructing entry to his premises, as he had been standing with a vehicle in front of his neighbour's shop. Two police officers were called by the defence, but said they saw no assault being committed. One, Constable William Bollington, said that Emanuel was 'cool, calm and collected', but Goodstone was standing in the crowd, shaking his hands, and jumping about on the pavement. In summing up, the chairman said that the defendant had no right to invite a man into his shop and assault him in such an undignified way as he had done. To mark his sense of the indignity that had been put upon 'a poor man', he was imposing a fine of £2, plus £1 16s costs, against the defendant.

1883   John Ryan, of Southampton Row, Portsea, assaulted Mrs Rose Bright, and caused wilful damage to the amount of £1 8s. He lived next door to her, and went into her house while he was drunk and struck her without provocation, then went upstairs and smashed a looking-glass, table, washstand, and several other pieces of furniture. When he was charged at Portsmouth Police Court on 6 June, he said in his defence that the beer which had made him drunk was sold to him by the complainant. He was fined £1 16s, including costs, or seven days' imprisonment.   30 MAY

31 MAY

1847 John Gregory, an engine driver, aged about 28, was killed on the Portsmouth branch of the London and Brighton railway. He was driving the 4.10 from Brighton to Bosham, which arrived on schedule at 5.40 p.m. and then started for the rest of the journey to Havant. It was travelling at about 30-35mph when the engine ran off the line about a mile from Emsworth, dragging after it the tender and the luggage van next to it. The connecting bar which linked the engine to the tender was broken, and the engine came off at an angle of 45 degrees, ran across the up line, breaking and tearing the rails, and went over the embankment, about 4ft deep, with a ditch at the bottom. The engine turned upside down and stuck, and the impetus of the train drove the fore part of the luggage van right upon the tender, stuck there fast, and prevented the train from proceeding any further. None of the passengers were hurt, and they alighted to find the engine driver and his stoker, Joseph Peel, lying across the rails under the foremost carriage. One of Gregory's legs had been severed from his body, probably by the wheel of the tender passing over it. His body was doubled up and mangled. Peel was lying next to him, one of his arms having been severed in the accident. The surgeons thought he was unlikely to survive, and after hospital treatment he was admitted to Bethnal Green lunatic asylum. He never recovered his reason.

JUNE

Andover High Street, the scene of riots in June 1914. (*Mary Evans Picture Library*)

1 JUNE

1934 The General Medical Council directed the removal from the Register of the name of Hugh Percival Francis Modder, registered as of Southampton Borough Hospital. In October 1933, he had been committed for trial by Southampton Magistrates Court for attempting suicide by morphia injections, and using certain instruments on Miss Mary Rennie Templeton, a nurse from Highcliffe, in order to procure a miscarriage; both offences had been committed in the previous month. He appeared at Winchester Assizes on 12 December, was found guilty on both counts, and was sentenced to six months for unlawfully using an instrument and twenty-one days for the suicide attempt, both sentences to run concurrently.

2 JUNE

1888 Henry Boyce was seen engaged in 'furious riding' on Southsea Common, and appeared at Portsmouth Police Court on 11 June. After the Queen's birthday parade of troops, he rode across the common on horseback at the rate of about 12mph. There was a large crowd of homeward-bound spectators there and the horse struck the right arm of Caroline Manning, who was pushing a perambulator. Her arm was broken, and the force of the collision threw the horse down. Mrs Manning went at once to Landport Hospital. Boyce said that as he was riding quietly on the Common, a stone was thrown at his horse, which immediately galloped off, and before he could stop it the accident occurred. He was fined 15s, including 3s costs.

Southsea Common, scene of Henry Boyce's 'furious ride' on 2 June 1888.

Southsea Common from Clarence Pier.

1874 Charles Giles (48) was charged with indecently exposing himself at the People's Park, Landport, with intent to insult Frances Ogburn (3) on the previous evening. She had been playing with other children on the swings, when the prisoner stood in front of them committing the offence, 'continuing his filthy conduct for some time'. When she got home she told her father, and two other children present later gave corroborative evidence. Annie Peachey said she saw the prisoner watching the children for some time, and after what the children told her he had been doing, she threw a stone at him. For the defence, Mr Ford said he was of previous good character, and he could produce medical evidence to confirm that he was suffering from a disease which could on occasion make him look as if he was behaving indecently. The magistrates said there was not enough evidence to convict him, and he was discharged.

3 JUNE

1914 Lieutenant Thomas Creswell, an experienced pilot, and Commander Arthur Rice, on the staff of the War College at Portsmouth, accompanying him as a passenger, left Calshot Air Station on a seaplane at about 4 p.m., carried out manoeuvres over Southampton Water, but on their return flight the machine was seen to fall into the water from a height of about 500ft. It sank almost immediately: both officers were drowned and the machine was wrecked. The accident was observed from the air station and assistance was sent at once. When the wreckage was drawn to the surface, Creswell's body was found inside, but Rice's body was never recovered. To date, this was one of the few fatal air accidents to have occurred since the establishment of the naval wing of the Royal Flying Corps. Unlike the army, the navy had been relatively immune from such occurrences.

4 JUNE

1878 An inquest was held at the Fox Inn, Bournemouth, on the body of Luke James (42), a labourer who had perished whilst he was trying to jump aboard a horse-drawn cart laden with gravel. He missed his footing, fell underneath, and one of the wheels passed over him, killing him instantly. A verdict of accidental death was recorded.

5 JUNE

1927 Richard Randal, a patient at Knowle Mental Hospital, near Fareham, who was allowed to patrol the grounds, was knocked over by a passing train and found dead on the railway line.

6 JUNE

1935 Percy Charles Brading (44) shot himself dead at his home in Drill Hall Road, Newport, on the day of his father's funeral. Before turning the gun on himself, he had fired at Mr Abraham Davies, the executor under his father's will and his father's second wife's brother, who had called to see him about the estate. Mr Davies could not attend the inquest on 11 June as he was in hospital, suffering from two slight bullet wounds in the head and cuts on the hands caused when he jumped through a window of the room where the attack was made on him. Police Sergeant Denness, who called on Brading after Davies had been brought to the police station, and had reported the shooting, said he had found six empty cartridge cases. Brading had

7 JUNE

evidently emptied a revolver at Davies before reloading it to shoot himself. The dead man's widow said her husband had been unable to work since being injured in a motorcycling accident the previous year, but denied they were in abject poverty. When he heard he had been left out of his father's will he was very upset, but afterwards said he did not care. He and his father had been on bad terms, had quarrelled and were not on speaking terms. She added that those who benefited under the will proposed to make her husband a gift of £500. Ten years earlier, he had tried to commit suicide by gas poisoning.

Lieutenant-Colonel H.G. Thomson, under whom Brading had served in the 5th Hampshire Howitzer Battery during the war, said that Brading had taken part in the Mesopotamian campaign of 1915-6, had been captured, and endured terrible hardships of captivity for three years. Of 126 men of his battery captured in Kut, he was one of only thirty-six survivors by the time of the Armistice. The coroner said that the deceased had evidently brooded over being left out of the will, and intended to kill Davies. The ammunition was old and faulty, and this had probably saved Davies's life. In his temper and frustration, Brading turned the weapon on himself.

8 JUNE   1958   Mr R. Formby, a farmer at Tidworth, drowned when his rowing boat overturned on the Thames at Pangbourne, Berkshire. His wife and children, aged six and eleven, were rescued.

9 JUNE   1876   An inquiry was held at Eastney Barracks into the recent death of John French, aged about 21, a gunner in the Royal Marine Artillery. Gunner George Pinfold identified the body of French, who had hired a boat on Southsea beach at about 3.30 p.m. on 21 May, and with witness and two friends had sailed up Portsmouth harbour. When they returned to the beach about an hour and a half later, the boat capsized. All four passengers fell into the water, and on

Southsea Beach and pier, where French and his friends had hired their boat.

coming up to the surface, they clung to the side of the boat for a while. Three were rescued, by a pleasure boat and steamer respectively, but there was no sign of French at first. His body was washed ashore later that day. When he was questioned by the coroner, who asked whether any of them understood about the management of a boat, Pinfold said that they 'all understood it a little', but they did not sail at all though they could all row. He did not know whether French could swim, but felt confident that the boat was perfectly safe for four persons. The weather conditions had been fine, with good visibility and only a mild breeze. They had all had a little beer to drink beforehand, but were perfectly sober at the time of the accident, and he denied that they had been 'skylarking', only changing positions in the boat. A verdict of accidental death was returned.

Eastney Barracks, Portsmouth, scene of an enquiry into the drowning of gunner John French in June 1876.

1887   Charles Taylor (20) was killed on the Fareham and Netley railway. At an inquest the next day at the Wheatsheaf, Titchfield, men who had been working with him said that they were engaged in loading wagons in Park cutting at about 9.30 p.m. when suddenly a large quantity of earth fell over, and he was killed when it threw him against the side of the truck.

10 JUNE

1848   William Alter, a convict at Portsmouth, struck James O'Connor, his superintendent, in the face with a mallet. A group of other convicts who were standing around picked up the injured man, bleeding profusely around the head and face, and took him to the Star Inn. The next day he became delirious, before falling into a coma and dying later that night. Alter remarked, 'I told him I would cook his goose, and I have done it.' He was taken into custody, and placed in a solitary cell on board the *York* convict ship. He dictated a written statement, saying that O'Connor had got him into trouble by threatening to report him for using threatening language, and worked him into such a state of madness that he did not know what he was doing. He was tried for wilful murder at Winchester Assizes in July and sentenced to be hanged.

11 JUNE

1863   The body of a newly-born girl was found in a slop pail near one of the lavatories attached to the House of Industry at Newport. Susan Dore, who was cook to the Revd Mr Elger, the chaplain, admitted responsibility. After giving birth, she sent for Mrs Elger, who saw that she was in pain. When she asked what the matter was, Miss Dore confessed all; 'Oh, ma'am, I have had a child, and I deserve hanging, for nothing is too bad for me.' Mrs Elger asked where the child was, and the cook showed her the body. A doctor was sent for, but the baby was dead. He thought it must have been suffocated at birth, as there were no signs of violence on the body. An inquest the next day recorded an open verdict to the effect that the infant was born alive, but there was no evidence as to whether its death was an accident or had been caused by violence.

12 JUNE

13 JUNE

1934 Basil Arthur Savill Young (54) appeared on remand before the magistrates at Alresford, charged with attempting to murder Bernard Johnston St Foyne Fair at his home at Bishop's Sutton. Young had been manager of Associated Estancias Ltd, London, in South America, and Fair was chairman. In August 1933 Young had made a complaint against the board and told the secretary, Owen Downing, that he intended to pursue claims he had made, and would go on until he had paid Fair 'in body, blood and soul'. On 30 May, Young visited Fair at his home, and asked him when he was going to repay the money he owed him. Downing said he did not owe Young anything, and Young became excited and started screaming. Fair tried to pacify him, advising him to bring an action against the company if he had any legal claim. Young replied, 'very well,' put his hand in his pocket, drew out a revolver and fired at Fair. The bullet missed him and became embedded in the woodwork of the window. Young was tried at Winchester Assizes on 6 July and found not guilty of shooting with intent to murder, but guilty of shooting with intent to do grievous bodily harm. A medical officer at Winchester Gaol said he was satisfied Young was insane at the time, and the judged ordered his detention during His Majesty's pleasure.

14 JUNE

1897 The mail steamer *Scot* arrived at Southampton, with the body of Barney Barnato (46), a diamond merchant and financier, on board. Barnato, born in London, had made his fortune largely in South Africa, but after a series of setbacks in around 1895 he took to drinking heavily, and showed evidence of mental instability and paranoia. He was sailing home to attend the celebrations for Queen Victoria's Diamond Jubilee, and though he seemed in good spirits on board, he was under regular surveillance. On 14 June, as the ship was nearing Madeira, he was walking on board, leaning on a fellow passenger's arm. Suddenly, without warning, he wrenched his arm away and threw himself overboard. A senior officer plunged in to try and rescue him. He himself had to be rescued when a boat was lowered, and Barnato's body was recovered, floating head downwards. A verdict of suicide was recorded at the inquest.

15 JUNE

1801 Mr Beazley and Mr Strickland, both from Ryde, were taking a passenger on board their boat. The passenger stood up in the boat during a sudden gust of wind, overturning it, and all three were drowned.

16 JUNE

1878 John Talbot, a stoker with HMS *Sultan*, which had served successively in the Channel and Mediterranean fleets, died in the Royal Naval Hospital, Haslar. He had been discharged from the hospital on Friday 14 June, and on the following evening he went to an inn in Portsea to ask whether he could have lodgings until Monday. Although he was sober at the time, it was thought that he looked unwell; he said he had been invalided home because of a foot injury. Later in the evening, he was seen with his head resting on the table. During the night he was sick; by 8.30 the next morning he was in a coma. He was taken back to hospital, but died later in the day. A post-mortem examination showed he was suffering from congestion of the brain,

HMS *Sultan*.
John Talbot, a
stoker on board,
died suddenly in
June 1878.

and intense and extensive congestion of the lungs, the latter being sufficient
to cause death.

1956 Albert Goozee took Lydia Leakey and her 14-year-old daughter Norma   17 JUNE
from their home in Poole for a picnic in the New Forest. Goozee had been Mr
and Mrs Leakey's lodger since January 1955, but Tom Leakey was disabled
and before long his wife and Goozee were having an affair. He later claimed,
probably without foundation, that at one stage Norma also wanted 'the same
attentions' from him that her mother was getting. After an argument and
violent struggle at the picnic scene, Goozee drove away, leaving mother and
daughter both dead. He was arrested and charged with murder, and went
on trial at Winchester Assizes in December, where he pleaded not guilty to
murdering Norma Leakey. The jury decided otherwise. He was sentenced to
death. but reprieved two hours before the time scheduled for his execution.
Diagnosed as a paranoid schizophrenic, he was sent to Broadmoor for life.
Released on licence in 1971, he was imprisoned again in 1982 for stabbing
and wounding a neighbour, set free again in 1993 but was back in court and
custody again three years later for sexually assaulting two girls aged 12 and
13.

1890 Edwin Ruddiford (73) of Colebrook Place, Winchester, killed himself.   18 JUNE
A pensioner from the 46th Foot Regiment, Duke of Cornwall Infantry, since
leaving the service he had sold pies at street corners, and was known as 'Jimmy
the Pieman'. About fourteen years earlier, he had had 'a paralytic seizure in
the head', and since then, according to his widow, had been 'a mere shipwreck
of his former self'. For the last two years he had been subject to attacks of
erysipelas, and on the previous day told her he feared he was about to have
another attack. If the pain continued any more, he warned her, he would go
mad. In the afternoon Mrs Ruddiford went to buy some faggots, leaving him
in bed. When she returned, she found he had gone into the next room, cut his

throat with a razor, and was lying dead on the floor in a pool of blood. At the inquest at the Guildhall on 19 June, Dr Earle, who carried out the post-mortem, said he could not have survived for more than three minutes after inflicting the wounds on himself. A verdict of suicide while of unsound mind was recorded.

19 JUNE

1914 For two or three days Andover was the scene of riots, destruction of property and scuffles with police. It began in the evening when several hundred people gathered at the town station to meet the train from Winchester bringing a woman and her daughter who had been released from gaol after imprisonment for non-payment of a fine for assault on another resident. The crowd escorted the discharged persons to a shop and began breaking windows. These were barricaded, and a force of foot and mounted Hampshire police was drafted into the town.

On the morning of 20 June, an angry crowd gathered at the top of High Street, jeering the police and throwing stones at windows. The police tried but failed to move the crowd on by peaceable means. At midnight, further drafts of police were summoned to begin clearing the upper part of the street. The sullen crowd resisted, and as they were forced along Newbury Street they pelted the police with stones, brickbats, and other missiles. The police drew their batons and mounted, charging up High Street, but they still could not clear the street until 2 a.m. on Sunday. Riots resumed in the afternoon, and the crowd marched along Marlborough Street to Junction Station, smashing lamps and windows as they went. About 2,000 men and women, mostly young, were thought to have been involved. On the previous night the fronts of most of the tradesmen's shops were smashed, and the trail of destruction continued that night. Between 10 p.m. and 11 p.m., stones and brickbats were thrown at the vicarage, and most of the windows were broken. The church opposite was locked early in the evening, and nobody attempted to damage it. One of the houses attacked was owned by Mr Beale, one of the magistrates who had imposed the fine on the girl and her mother. Public houses were closed by 9 p.m., and windows were barricaded. The Chief Constable of Hampshire asked everyone to be in their houses by 10 p.m. The crowd had not dispersed by 12.30 a.m. on Sunday, and in High Street constables with drawn truncheons were seen chasing people who still defied the request. During the day the unrest died down, but several constables and members of the public had been injured, and a woman was admitted to hospital with cuts on the face and a fractured skull.

20 JUNE

1913 Harry Blaker (17) was tried at Winchester Assizes and found guilty of the murder of his grandfather, Frederick Ridges (59), a widower, at Southampton, on 8 March. They had lived together for about fourteen years, and after some disagreement Blaker struck his grandfather with a hammer while he lay sleeping. The defence argued that the youth was mentally defective, and in returning their verdict the jury recommended him to mercy. Mr Justice Ridley passed sentence of death, which was later commuted to detention during His Majesty's pleasure.

1931 Hubert Chevis (28), a Lieutenant of the 15th Light Battery of the Royal
Artillery, died in hospital at Frimley. He and his wife Frances had had a meal
of partridge and vegetables at their rented bungalow near Blackdown Camp,
Aldershot, the previous evening, but complained that the meat tasted terrible.
Both experienced a burning sensation
at the back of their throats and were
sent to hospital, but while Frances
soon recovered, Hubert had severe
convulsions, and stopped breathing
at around midnight. Despite efforts to
revive him, he was pronounced dead
about ten hours later.

On 24 June, the day of Hubert's
funeral, his father, Sir William, at
Bournemouth received an unsigned
telegram reading 'Hooray, Hooray,
hooray'. The original of the telegram
was found to have the signature of a
J. Hartigan. A photograph of it was published in the press a   Blackdown Camp,
week later with an appeal for assistance, and the newspaper's editor received   Aldershot, where
a postcard asking why he had published it, signed – again – J. Hartigan. The   Lieutenant Hubert
inquest established that Mr Chevis had died from asphyxiation as a result of   Chevis was fatally
strychnine poisoning, but whether he had been murdered, attempted suicide,   poisoned in June
or whether it was negligence on the part of the partridges' suppliers, was never   1931. (© *Nicola Sly*)
established. A further postcard was received by Sir William Chevis, reading, 'A
mystery they will never solve. J. Hartigan. Hooray.' The mysterious Hartigan
was right; it was never solved, and he or she was never traced.

1862 Mary Hall (23), of Fordingbridge, left her father William's farm in
the morning, as usual, to attend morning service at St Mary's church. That
afternoon her body was found in a ditch on the farm boundary. She had been
strangled until she was unconscious and then placed face down in the ditch
to drown. Only four days earlier, she had told her father and stepmother
that she dreamed she was being put to death by somebody who would
not give her time to say her prayers first. George Gilbert, who lived about 500yds
away, and who had worked briefly as a labourer on the farm, was arrested and
charged with her murder. He was a habitual petty criminal who had served
sentences for burglary and had been transported for attacking a woman, and
whose unwanted attentions to Mary made her avoid him as much as possible.

Although he pleaded not guilty, and though the evidence was largely
circumstantial, the prosecution produced twenty-two witnesses at his trial at
Winchester Assizes on 18 July. The defence could not produce one. The jury
found him guilty and he was hanged by William Calcraft on 4 August. Several
months later, hidden in the thatched roof of Gilbert's cottage, a workman
found items of jewellery that Mary Hall had been wearing on the day she
was killed. By this time her father had died, supposedly of a broken heart.

23 JUNE **1861** An altercation took place between four drunken women in a house in Kent Street, Portsea. It started with a quarrel over a man with whom one was acquainted. Two of the women, Harriet Ferguson and Eliza Slepe, attacked another, Julia Vaughan, who ran upstairs to get away from them. Shortly afterwards, Vaughan was seen to fall out of the window, about 9ft from the ground. She had apparently jumped out to escape from them, and as she did so one of them stabbed her in the thigh. Dr Jackson, who fortunately happened to be passing at the time, ordered her immediate removal to hospital. When she was examined, it was found that the hamstrings of the right thigh had been severed. She reported the behaviour of Slepe and Ferguson, who were arrested and remanded in custody.

24 JUNE **1834** A prize fight took place between Owen Swift and Anthony Noon, both aged about 23, in a field about four miles from Andover, for £50 a side. The fight had lasted about two hours. Then, Swift landed a tremendous blow on the throat of his adversary, a strike which threw him to the ground and onto the back of his head. As he did not get up at once, the contest was declared in favour of Swift. Noon was taken to Andover and was put to bed, but after two or three hours of severe pain he died. Before the fight had begun, he had declared that he would either win, 'or die in the ring'. He left a wife and two children. It was noted that once the men who attended the fight heard that there were concerns about his condition, they made themselves scarce, apparently content to let him fend for himself. A large number of women had also been watching the fight, and it was presumably one or more of them who looked after him once he had been knocked out.

25 JUNE **1832** The *Times* reported on what it called the 'extraordinary' instances of soldiers attempting suicide, either to avoid flogging or even a drill punishment. Two recent cases which had come to light concerned soldiers: one, of the 33rd

Clarence Road Barracks. In 1832, the authorities were alarmed by the extent of self-harm by soldiers at such establishments throughout Hampshire. (© *Diane Webb*)

Regiment at Forton Barracks, Gosport, cut his throat and died immediately; on the same day, a soldier of the 14th Regiment blew his hand off in the Cambridge Barracks, Portsmouth, with his own musket whilst on the open parade. Although he survived, the bone of the arm was so badly shattered that the entire limb had to be amputated.

26 JUNE **1966** Stephen Eldridge-Quick (15), a pupil at Bembridge School, was killed when he fell while trying to scale the 250ft cliff at Whitecliff, Bembridge. His companion, a boy two years older from the same school, climbed down and tried to rescue him, but there was nothing he could do. An RAF helicopter airlifted Stephen to hospital at Newport, but he was pronounced dead on arrival.

1870 James Thompson (50), a gardener, allegedly shot at his wife Ann at Whippingham,and threatened to kill her. She had lived in his house as his housekeeper for some time before their marriage in January. On 23 July, she told him she wanted to go to a rose show, but he told her she had to get his dinner first. When he came home from work he swore at her, followed her upstairs, pulled off part of her dress, locked up her hat, and said she would not go. When she asked him to give her the key, he told her that if she got it he would stab her, at which she picked up her clothes and went to her mother's house next door. On 26 July, he accused her of taking his revolver and bank book out of the house behind his back, and of seeing other men. When she came home the next day her husband came out of the door to meet her. She asked, 'What do you mean by saying I have men in the house?' At this, he allegedly put his hand in his pocket, drew out a revolver, and fired at her. They were only six yards apart, but the bullet whizzed past her and hit the hedge instead. 'Stand aside, or I'll kill you,' he threatened.

When he was tried at Winchester Assizes on 14 July, she described under cross-examination how she had followed him down the road, asking the names of the witnesses who claimed she had men at home. The judge pointed out that she did this after he had apparently threatened to murder her; did she ask for assistance? She admitted she did not. A witness said that Mr Thompson merely fired at a tree, not at his wife, and the defence said he merely fired in order to empty the barrels. In summing up, the judge said that to fire a pistol to frighten a timid person was a misdemeanour punishable by twenty years' penal servitude, but in this case the evidence was too weak and Thompson was discharged.

1871 William Henry Carpenter (4), of Standford Street, Southampton, was accidentally poisoned. His mother Anne was working at the Melbourne Arms while her son and three other boys were playing in the yard. She heard a scream, and when she went out she found some liquid in his mouth that looked just like milk. She wiped it off, and then the children told her he had drunk something out of a small bottle (which they found afterwards). A neighbour advised her to administer salt and water to make him sick, and she did so; she then took him to Mr Bencraft, who gave him an antidote. However, the child was in increasing agony, and there was little the doctor could do but look after him and try to make him as comfortable as possible. He died on 4 July.

An inquest was held later that day at the Apollo Tap, Chapel Road. A labourer, Edwin Lilly, said he had bought some aqua-fortis and quicksilver from a local chemist, put them in a bottle, clearly marked 'Poison', with some water, and used it at the Melbourne Arms when helping the landlord to clean his harnesses. One of the boys had evidently taken the bottle from the shelf. In accepting the jury's verdict of 'death by accidental poisoning', the coroner remarked that as far as he could see, nobody was to blame.

1964 Michael Szczap (12) went to use the lavatory on the 3.25 p.m. Southampton to Reading train shortly after it had pulled out of Basingstoke. On the floor he found the dead body of Yvonne Patricia Laker (15), a schoolgirl whose father was an RAF serviceman stationed in Singapore. She had been

Basingstoke Station. The dead body of Yvonne Laker was discovered in the lavatory of a train that left this station in June 1964. (© Nicola Sly)

struck over the left eye with a sherry bottle, and the broken glass had been used to cut her throat. Her knees and feet were dirty, suggesting that she had been dragged some distance along the corridor. The other train passengers, who must have included the murderer and witnesses, were quickly moved on to another train, with no effort having been made to take their names and addresses first. The lavatory was scrubbed clean, removing all bloodstains and fingerprints, while Yvonne's body was wrapped in a couple of blankets before being sent to the mortuary. When the police were called to investigate the murder, they were furious that so much valuable forensic evidence had been destroyed.

Derek Pye (27), an unemployed farm labourer, who had been travelling on the same train, was arrested three days later, and charged with her murder. He denied having any involvement with the case, but went on trial at Winchester Assizes on 23 November. The evidence against him was largely circumstantial, and with the loss of so much vital evidence on the train immediately after the murder, the prosecution's case was seriously weakened. He was found not guilty of the killing and acquitted. However, he had already had three previous convictions, two for larceny and one for assault. He was found guilty of committing most of the offences, and sentenced to eighteen months' imprisonment. Nobody was ever brought to justice for Yvonne Laker's death.

30 JUNE

1939 An inquest was held at Portsmouth on the body of Lieutenant-Commander William Wood (36), who had been found dead in his cabin on HMS *Hood*. A verdict of suicide was returned.

JULY

The Duke of Monmouth flees the field at Sedgemoor, July 1865,
escapes and seeks refuge at Ringwood.

1 JULY   **1954** Captain Edward Baxter (46), of No. 245 Armament Battery, Royal Artillery, Gosport, was found dead in a locked public convenience near Gosport ferry. He had a knife wound in his chest, and a note was found beside him.

2 JULY   **1902** William Churcher (35), of Clarence Buildings, Gosport, was tried at Winchester Assizes for the wilful murder of Sophia Hepworth (30). She was separated from her husband, and had lived with Churcher for several years. She had been a heavy drinker, and one evening she ran down the street, falling in the river. He was arriving home from work at the time, rescued her from the water, took her home, and they had an argument about her love of the bottle. Particularly angry on this occasion – he said she had been an embarrassment to him – he took a knife and stabbed her thirty-three times. The police forced an entry into the house two days later and found her body sitting upright in a chair, covered in blood, and her head wrapped in a towel.

Churcher was arrested and committed to Portsmouth Gaol, and on 17 April he tried to kill himself by jumping overboard from the ferry launch while crossing the harbour in the company of two lawyers. Rescued and given restoratives, he recovered in time for the court proceedings at which he was charged with murder. At his trial he claimed that she had thrown a lamp and two vases at him before attacking him with a knife, and he was only acting in self-defence. However, it was pointed out that he had not reported the attack at the time but stayed in the house with her dead body for over 24 hours, and also that he had not mentioned any degree of provocation until the trial. Some of the neighbours testified that they had heard her begging him not to hurt her. The jury returned a verdict of guilty, but with a recommendation to mercy. It was disregarded, and he was hanged at Winchester on 22 July.

3 JULY   **1964** Douglas Wiltshire (48), a farmer and owner of three grocery shops in Southampton, claimed when he appeared at Winchester Assizes that a policeman had caused him serious bodily harm. On 17 December 1962, as he was returning to his home in Botley after an evening with fellow Rotarians, he was stopped and accused of speeding and driving after drinking. When he refused to get out of his car, Constable Dennis Barrett grabbed him around the throat, kicked and punched him, and repeatedly struck him with a truncheon. Dr Markham gave evidence that one wound on the leg, which needed stitching, was almost certainly caused by a blow from a blunt instrument. The hearing was adjourned and resumed until the following week. On 9 July the court found in his favour, and he was awarded damages of £589 17s 6d plus costs.

4 JULY   **1885** Isabella Easton (29), of Mary Street, Fratton, was charged with attempting to commit suicide. At about 8.55 a.m. she jumped into the water in Portsmouth Harbour, and was seen by Frederick Passels, an officer of the Old Steam Launch Co., who rescued her with a boathook. As she was brought back to land, she told him despairingly, 'Let me go – I mean doing it.' Dr Maybury had attended her recently and said she seemed very depressed. He had recently attended her for illness connected with her confinement, though reports did not specify whether she was still pregnant or had post-natal depression, and she was remanded for a week.

1825 Mary Ann Massell, a servant at Vincent Street, Westminster, answered 5 JULY
the door to find a man carrying a basket with a label addressed to her employer,
Mr Fricke. She paid the porter 2s as requested, and inspected the contents –
which gave off a terrible smell once she had removed several sheets of paper from
the top. Investigating further among the wrappings, she found to her horror the
dead body of a baby boy. She took it to a nearby surgeon, and police investigation
found that the parcel had arrived on the mail coach from Southampton a day
earlier. The handwriting on the label was traced to a Mr Higgs at the Black Swan,
Winchester.

   A police officer went to visit the town and found out that the baby was
probably one that had been born on 4 July to Jane Sturgess, a spinster living
with her mother in a cottage adjoining the cathedral. Although she was
suspected of murder and concealment, there was not enough information to
convict her, or even establish whether the infant was hers or not. Neither did
anyone solve the mystery of why it had been placed in a basket and sent to Mr
Fricker. The jury returned a verdict of 'wilful murder against some person or
persons unknown'.

1926 Charles Edward Finden (22) was sentenced to death at Winchester 6 JULY
Assizes at the end of a two-day trial for the murder of John Richard Thompson
(14). The boy had been working on a farm and disappeared shortly after
receiving his last wages. His body was found by two gypsies under a bush on
a piece of waste land beside the Alton to Basingstoke railway line, about half
a mile from his Alton home. He had been strangled with a necktie. Finden was
arrested on 24 June, and pleaded not guilty, claiming that he had been asleep
in a nearby fileld when the crime was committed. His wife testified that he had
given her a 10s note and two halfcrowns, which he claimed he had earned by
working at a local tennis court, but enquiries revealed that he had never been
employed there, and the money was found to be the wages which he had stolen
from his victim.

   Witnesses said they had seen Finden and another person in the meadow on
the afternoon before the killing, but thought they were merely bird-nesting.
He was hanged at Winchester Gaol on 12 August.

1945 A private court of inquiry in Aldershot sat to view reports of 7 JULY
disturbances by Canadian soldiers in the town during the last two evenings.
The incidents were thought to be the work of a few hotheads, and though
over 100 people had been held for questioning at the height of the trouble,
only half a dozen were still in custody. On the first night, 5 July, a gang
entered an amusement arcade, broke every automatic machine, threw some
into the street, overturned stationary cars, and smashed shop windows. All
the men involved were sober, but angry, discontented and impatient with
the delays which prevented them from going home. The trouble was even
worse on the following evening, when men surged through the town centre,
especially Wellington Street and Union Street, where not a single pane of
glass remained untouched. Some of them entered a brewery store and helped
themselves to beer and spirits. One Canadian military policeman hit a man

over the head with a bottle: and he ran into the streets, his face streaming with blood.

As most of the convoys left on 7 July, Lieutenant-General P.J. Montague, Chief of Staff at the Canadian Military Headquarters, expressed regret for injury done to the town by a small and irresponsible group whose 'senseless, cowardly action has earned them the contempt of the great majority of the Canadian army overseas'. He promised that the military authorities would make good the damage, estimated at over £10,000.

8 JULY

James, Duke of Monmouth, from an engraving after a painting by Sir Peter Lely.

1685 James, Duke of Monmouth, the illegitimate son of the late King Charles II, who had rebelled against the new sovereign, his uncle King James II, and whose motley army had been defeated in the Battle of Sedgemoor, escaped and took shelter in a house in West Street, Ringwood, now named Monmouth House. While there he wrote a letter to the King, begging for forgiveness. Another account says that he was found by the King's soldiers hiding in a ditch near Ringwood. Whichever version of events is true, he was captured and imprisoned in the Tower of London. An Act of Attainder for high treason had been passed against him, making a trial unnecessary, and he was beheaded later that month.

9 JULY

1897 Henry Smith (53), a Petersfield confectioner, was tried at Winchester Assizes for criminally assaulting his daughter, Flora (15), several times between November 1896 and January 1897. Mrs Smith had died three years previously, leaving him with several young daughters and a son. The prosecution alleged that after he had assaulted her, he forced her to write a letter denying that he had ever 'insulted' her in any way. At length she and her sister Alice could take no more, and late at night on 13 February they both left the house, went to a neighbour, and the police were alerted. Smith denied the allegations, saying that they were being made against him because they wanted to get their hands on his business for themselves. When cross-examined, he answered so many questions unsatisfactorily that his own counsel told him if he did not answer properly then he would no longer defend his case. Smith was found guilty and sentenced to fifteen years' penal servitude.

10 JULY

1928 An inquest was held on the body of Mrs Annie Neale (48) of Dover Road, Portsmouth, wife of an upholsterer. Not long before, an X-ray examination had revealed that she had an extra rib, and the doctors recommended an operation to have it removed. She was so worried at the thought of this that she poisoned herself. A verdict of suicide while of unsound mind was returned.

11 JULY

1932 John Parker (48), a painter, Alfred Hinds (43), a dealer, and Benjamin Bennett (30), a motor mechanic, were charged at Winchester Assizes with robbery and violence and the theft of £23,977 from Lloyds Bank, Portsmouth, on

Scenes from the Tower of London, where the Duke of Monmouth was imprisoned before his execution.

25 April. As the bank treasurer and a messenger were taking a bag containing the money to the post office, a car with four men inside pulled up. One man jumped out and struck down the messenger with a blunt instrument, snatched the bag, and the car drove away at great speed. All three were found guilty, and a police inspector proved several convictions against Parker, including one of burglary and wounding. Hinds also had similar convictions in the past, while Bennett had long since been suspected by Scotland Yard of the driver of cars used in several smash and grab raids. Parker was sentenced to five years' penal servitude, Hinds to four, Bennett to three, and each was ordered to receive fifteen strokes of the 'cat'.

12 JULY

1960   A Southampton boy of 11 was charged at Winchester Assizes with murdering Iris Margaret Dawkins (9), inflicting thirty-nine stab wounds on her while they were playing cowboys and Indians with other children in Mayfield Park on 20 February. He pleaded not guilty, and had told the police that, 'I have seen stabbing on television and next week you see them in another part'. He was discharged the following day.

In November 1968 Keith Ridley (22), a bookkeeper of Southampton, was seen loitering with a sheath knife on him. When arrested, he admitted to police that he had the urge to kill every so often and he had come out with a knife, intending to do away with somebody. He also admitted killing Iris Dawkins in 1960. (Assuming his age was given correctly in the 1968 newspaper report, he would have actually been 13 or 14 at his original trial.). Despite having been discharged on the previous occasion, he appeared in court at Winchester again in March. The defence maintained that there was no evidence with which to convict him, and one would have to go back many centuries to find a situation where the jury was asked to investigate a murder nine years old when the only evidence available was a confession. Nevertheless, the jury found him guilty, and he was sentenced to be detained at Her Majesty's pleasure.

13 JULY

1961   An inquest on Captain Eric Vivian (69), RN (Retd), returned a verdict of suicide while the balance of his mind was disturbed. On 9 July he was found dying from gunshot wounds at his Hambledon home. His wife, and one of their three sons, had woken just before 4.30 a.m. to hear a shot, and found him lying in his pyjamas on the front lawn. His 12-bore shotgun was by his side. He died soon after being admitted to the Royal Portsmouth Hospital.

14 JULY

1801   A boy gathering cherries near Itchen Ferry fell from the tree, and landed on his head. He broke his back, his legs were paralysed, and he died a few days later.

15 JULY

1873   Matthew Keogh was indicted at Winchester Assizes before Mr Fitzjames Stephen, for the wilful murder of Hans Bjerritz, a Danish citizen, on the High Seas. Keogh, his wife and the deceased were passengers on board the mail steamer *Olbers*, from the River Plate to Southampton. Some disagreement had arisen between the men about berth accommodation, and on 21 March Bjerritz struck Keogh with a wooden baton. A drunken Keogh stabbed his attacker with a Spanish knife, and Bjerritz died that evening. The defence argued that the blow had been provocation enough, which the jury admitted, passing a verdict of manslaughter. After he was given a sentence of twenty years' penal servitude, Keogh was told that had there been a stricter interpretation of law, he would have been found guilty of murder.

1860 Sergeant Michael Hynes (32) of the 16th Foot Regiment, Aldershot, was **16 JULY** charged at Winchester Assizes with murder at Gosport on 9 March. While he was on leave, he stayed with his father-in-law, Mr John Clarke, a waterman who lived at Chapman's Yard, off High Street, Gosport. Some months earlier he had been wounded in the head, and taken to drinking heavily. After visiting several inns with a group of friends, he came back to the house at 7 p.m., rather the worse for wear. Mrs Clarke tried to persuade him to stay indoors for the rest of the evening, but he insisted on going out again. Mr Clarke went with him, to try and keep him out of trouble.

However, they met a friend in town who invited  them to the Rummor Inn, where Hynes had at least one glass of beer, four gins and a whisky. By the time Clarke got him home again he was extremely drunk, and argued with his parents-in-law, resulting in him and Mr Clarke coming to blows. Mr Clarke then ran for a policeman; both men then returned to the house. Meanwhile, Hynes took down his sword. Mrs Clarke asked her neighbour, Mrs Ann Shein (64), for help: the latter came in and tried to calm Hynes down, but he pushed Mrs Clarke outside and locked the front door. Her daughter Sarah (16) saw Hynes with his sword unsheathed: she ran upstairs and called out

Judge Sir James Fitzjames-Stephens, who presided over the trial of Matthew Keogh in July 1873.

loudly for help, then jumped out of the window into the street. Several other people in the street came and looked through the window, where they could see Hynes hacking at Mrs Shein. She died from her injuries two months later. After the post-mortem and inquest, the charge against Hynes of 'cutting and wounding with intent to murder' was changed to one of wilful murder.

At the trial, the jury were initially unsure whether Mrs Shein's death resulted from her wounds, coming as it did so long after the attack, but Mr Justice Keating said he was satisfied it did. They returned a verdict of guilty, but with a recommendation to mercy. The judge sentenced Hynes to death, but shortly before the date for his execution, 2 August, the sentence was commuted to life imprisonment.

Sergeant Hynes' head injuries were said to have contributed to his violent and unpredictable behaviour.

17 JULY

1860 William Henry Whitworth (39), a sergeant in the Royal Artillery, was charged at Winchester Assizes with the murder of his wife Martha, and their six young children, Mary Ann (11), Elizabeth (9), Frederick (6), Ellen (4), William (3), and Robert (16 months). On 18 May, he had run across the parade ground at Sandown Fort, and thrown himself on his knees before a captain, exclaiming, 'For God's sake, sir, save me!' He handed his watch, some papers and money to the captain, adding, 'He's used me dreadfully! He's held a pistol at my head, and swore he'd shoot me if I didn't cut my throat.' He then opened his coat to reveal the wound on his throat, saying, 'There's awful work down there! Pray go down!' After he was sent to the hospital, his living quarters were checked, and bloodstained footprints were found over much of the house. Tracks on the stair suggested that the children must have escaped from their bedroom, tried to run downstairs but were instead pursued back to the bedroom. The floor of the upper room was covered with blood, papers, and clothing, and among other articles found were a razor and cutlass with which the killings had obviously been carried out. On one of the beds was the body of Mrs Whitworth, her neck so badly gashed that the vertebra of the neck was clearly visible. The bodies of the children lay nearby, each with several wounds, and pillows had been used to stifle their cries.

Sandown esplanade in about 1924, close to the scene where the deranged Sergeant William Whitworth killed several members of his family in July 1860.

During his appearance in court Whitworth stared vacantly around the room, muttering some incoherent sentences, and at times he appeared to be chewing something. At one point he put his arm around the turnkey who was in charge

of him, smiled inanely and pointed at Mr Justice Keating. The doctor said that his mental powers 'were entirely gone', and after an address from the judge, the jury found that the prisoner was unable to plead. The judge then said that he would direct 'the usual order to be made'. When the gaoler motioned to Whitworth to leave the bar he was unable to understand, and when led away he cried out, 'Gracious God, look down upon you all, miserable sinners.'

18 JULY

1850 Master Gale, aged about two, of Southampton, pulled a dish of hot water from a kitchen shelf over his chest and scalded himself to death.

19 JULY

1545 The battle of the Solent was fought between the fleets of King Henry VIII and King Francis I of France. The latter had launched an invasion of England with 30,000 soldiers sailing in over 200 ships, which entered the Solent and landed troops on the Isle of Wight and the Sussex coast. On 18 July the English fleet left Portsmouth and engaged the French at long range, but with no real consequences for either side. Next day the French attacked the British ships, and as the *Mary Rose*, the flagship of Vice-Admiral Sir George Carew, advanced towards battle, she capsized and sank. Of the 500 men on board, only about twenty survived, Carew being one of those who was drowned.

Several reasons have been suggested for the cause of the disaster. The ship may have foundered because the crew did not close the lower gunports properly after firing at the galleys, so that when she was caught in a strong gust of wind she heeled, was flooded and turned over. Insubordination among the crew was also believed to be a factor, as was an epidemic of dysentery which would have left them unable to handle the battle properly. Alternatively, the vessel may have been unstable, gradually deteriorated over the years and become unseaworthy. Nevertheless, in maritime terms the battle proved inconclusive:, the French forces had gained no advantage, and returned to France in August.

King Henry VIII, whose fleet was engaged by the French at the battle of the Solent. Nearly 500 men were lost, but it ended in victory for neither side.

1869 Corporal James Brett, of the 2nd Battalion 7th Royal Fusiliers at Aldershot, was in charge of a regiment of soldiers who were meant to be emptying and refilling beds at the barrack stores. One of the men, Private William Dixon, was ordered to fill some extra beds, but objected on the grounds that he had already done more than his fare share of the work. Corporal Brett left to report Dixon's disobedience to a superior officer and, when he returned, Dixon picked up his rifle, aimed it and shot him, killing him instantly. After the bullet had gone through his head it went out of the window, narrowly missing some women in the married quarters in an adjacent hut. Dixon already had a reputation for surliness and insubordination, and had previously been court-martialled for lesser offences. After he was taken into custody and held at Winchester gaol awaiting trial, he told the deputy governor that Brett was always bullying him. At his trial on 18 August he was sentenced to death, and hanged on 6 September.

20 JULY

The murder of Corporal James Brett at Aldershot camp in July 1869. *(Illustrated Police News)*

MURDER AT ALDERSHOT CAMP

21 JULY

1683 William, Lord Russell, who had lived at East Stratton since 1667, was executed for his part in the Rye House plot, a conspiracy which involved an attempt to ambush and capture King Charles II and his heir James, Duke of York, while on their way back to London from the Newmarket races. Several others who had been similarly involved took the precaution of escaping to Holland, but he refused to join them. On 26 June he was sent to the Tower of London, and at his trial he was accused of promising assistance to rebels, planning to put himself at the head of a rebellion and attempting to bring about the King's death. He was convicted of treason and beheaded at Lincoln's Inn Fields. The Whigs revered his memory as a martyr, and claimed he had been made an example of through his efforts to exclude the Duke of York from the succession to the throne. When William III became King, he was posthumously pardoned by a reversal of attainder.

Left: William, Lord Russell, executed after the Rye House plot in 1683.

Right: William, Lord Russell's last farewell to his family before he went to the scaffold.

22 JULY

1955 John Armstrong, a sick-berth attendant at the Royal Naval Hospital, Haslar and his wife Janet, who lived at Southsea, called Dr Bernard Johnson of Portsmouth to attend to their ailing 5½-month-old son Terence, who was badly off colour and difficult to rouse. By the time the doctor arrived, the infant was dead. The doctor said he would be unable to issue a death certificate as the death was so sudden, and was surprised to observe that the parents did not seem particularly upset. A post-mortem revealed traces of poison in the stomach, which were at first thought to be poisoned berries which the baby's three-year-old sister Pamela might have offered him as 'sweeties', but on analysis they were found to be Seconal, a barbiturate used for treating severe insomnia. Another of the couple's children, Philip, had died at the age of nine weeks in March 1954, and on police instructions his body was exhumed at Southsea Cemetery to check for poison, but it was too badly decomposed to examine. Despite the police's suspicions of unlawful killing, there was insufficient evidence to charge either parent.

Shortly afterwards, the family moved to Gosport. In July 1956, the parents parted company, and Mrs Armstrong applied for a separation order and maintenance. She then made and signed a statement to the police, in which she admitted that she had thrown some Seconal capsules away on her husband's orders shortly after Terence's death. Both were charged with murder and went on trial at Winchester Assizes on 3 December. At the end of proceedings ten days later, Mrs Armstrong was found not guilty, but her husband was sentenced to death. He was due to be executed on 6 February 1957, but two days before the date, following an appeal, the Home Secretary recommended that he should be reprieved and sentenced to life imprisonment instead. Later, Mrs Armstrong admitted that she had given the baby Seconal to help him sleep. As she had already been tried and acquitted, she could not be tried again, but a campaign to have Mr Armstrong's sentence quashed in the light of his wife's statement did not succeed.

THE GHOST OF THE WHIMPERING DOG 23 JULY
The fifteenth-century Crown Inn, Alton, is said to be haunted by a dog which constantly whimpers and scratches. Legend has it that it is the ghost of an animal killed by its master, who had beaten it to death against the chimney breast in the dining room in a drunken rage. Though he had never seen it, a landlord in the mid-twentieth century reported that he had heard the ghost scratching, and once his two Pekinese dogs became quite frantic when they were near the chimney breast. During building work in 1967, workmen removed a false wall and revealed a canine skeleton near the original dining-room hearth.

1934 A week-long trial at Winchester Assizes of Edith Jane Creeth, 24 JULY postmistress of Brightstone, Isle of Wight, on charges of sending obscene and offensive literature through the post, was concluded. The letters had begun arriving in January 1930, and continued over the next three years; they were addressed to several different people in the area, and contained various threats, one reading, 'I smashed their windows. I would like to smash their heads, I have had some fun hearing all the police have had to say. You Hoopers are as crafty as monkeys, but can you tell who I am? I am making it damned hot for the post-office people.'

The case was based on the grounds of similarity of the handwriting to that of Mrs Creeth, and incidents which pointed to the inference that she was responsible for writing them. She herself claimed to have received some of them, containing attacks made on her and her mother in connection with the management of the post office, and said she had had windows smashed. Another recipient, Miss Willoughby, a schoolmistress, was so upset by them that she resigned her post. The counsel for the defence said that the 'wild' handwriting of the anonymous writer was very different from the neat, almost scholarly style of Mrs Creeth's known writing, that nobody would dare to convict solely on the shoddy evidence of handwriting, and that the letters had been deliberately posted while she was away, in order to incriminate her. She had pleaded not guilty; the jury agreed, and she was discharged.

25 JULY

1882 Ellen Dredge (23) tried to hang herself with a piece of rope at her mother's house in Collard's Court, Queen Street, Portsea. About two years earlier she had been married to a man who was subsequently convicted of bigamy, and ever since then she had suffered from depression. On the previous day, her mother had found her in the bedroom trying to kill herself by similar means. She was charged at Portsmouth Police Court on 26 July, and said that all she wanted to do was go home. The magistrates reminded her of 'the wicked act she had attempted', and remanded her in prison for an additional seven days, 'in order that she might receive the ministrations of the chaplain'.

26 JULY

1871 George Wilson, a blacksmith, attacked his wife Annie at Southampton. They had been separated for two years. On this day, she was in the company of a Mr Diaper in French Street when they met George. She thought he was about to go and chase after some girls, so she followed him in order to tell him not to. (Though as they had been separated for so long, one wonders what right she had to stop him, assuming his intentions were relatively innocent...) He remonstrated with her, but she kept following him; eventually, he lost patience with her, struck her in the chest, and she fell against the wall. Then he was seen to pick up a half-closed knife and hit her in the back of the head with it. When she went to Dr Palk, he found a raw incised wound in the back of her head. He was charged at Winchester Assizes on 13 December with feloniously wounding her, and admitted that he had thrown the knife at her that day. One of the witnesses for the defence was his brother-in-law, who described Annie Wilson as 'a very violent woman'. Although he had already been in prison for five months awaiting his court appearance, he was found guilty of unlawfully wounding her and sentenced to a further six months' with hard labour.

27 JULY

1588 Power magic was strongly associated with witchcraft, particularly in the medieval age. Its 'miraculous wind' is thought to have played a role in England's victory over the Spanish Armada in July 1588; according to legend the wind blew up after Hampshire witches met on an unknown site in the county to construct a 'cone of power' directed against the Spaniards. After it was formed, the witches converted it into a violent gale that divided and dispersed the enemy fleet. The wind chased the fleet up to the northern coast of Scotland, and then back down the Atlantic coast to Spain, so few ships were able to return home undamaged. More damage may have been caused by the

The Spanish Armada sailing up the Channel in crescent formation, from a sixteenth-century tapestry.

Battle is joined: a skirmish between the British and Spanish fleets rages off the south coast of England.

storm than action by English privateers. On 16 July, the English fleet was at Plymouth, awaiting news of the numerically superior Spanish force which had been delayed by bad weather and was sighted off the Cornish coast three days later. That evening, the English ships were trapped in Plymouth harbour by the incoming tide, while the Spanish convened a council of war, and decided to sail east towards the Isle of Wight. English ships set out from Plymouth, and over the next week there were two skirmishes before the final battle on 28 July which resulted in English victory over the Armada.

28 JULY

The Needles from Alum Bay, near which an unidentified man was killed in a yachting accident on 28 July 1963.

1963 When thick smoke was seen on the horizon just after midday by a coastguard at Southbourne, it gave the first hint of a yachting tragedy four miles west of the Needles in which a man was killed. Coastguards at the Needles directed the tanker *Esso Hythe* to the area, and radioed that the 25ft yacht *Maureen Grace*, registered at Southampton, was ablaze, with no trace of any survivors. The yacht burnt down to the water line and sank as the tanker searched the area. Two helicopters and four minesweepers joined various small craft taking part in the search, and after about two hours one of the helicopters picked up the body of a young man, landing it at Bournemouth. Nothing else was found, and after a few hours the search was called off.

29 JULY

1918 Albert Brook, a grocer from Bitterne, was fined £30 at Southampton for selling tobacco to which paper had been added. He bought cigarette ends picked up in the street at 4s per lb, added tobacco to them, and sold the result as 'ninepenny shag'.

Bitterne, where grocer Albert Brook was fined in July 1918.

1934   Alfred Seabrook (26), of Mile End, London, was run over by a trailer at   30 JULY
Portsdown Hill in the evening. He was taken to Portsmouth Hospital, where he
died of his injuries the next day.

1141   During most of the nineteen-year reign of King Stephen, between 1135   31 JULY
and 1154, he was locked in a struggle with his cousin 'Empress' Matilda,
daughter of the previous sovereign, King Henry I, who claimed that she was the
rightful monarch. The King's brother Henry, Bishop of Blois, sided with Matilda
and Earl Robert of Gloucester, agreeing to recognise her as Queen of England
on condition that she allowed him certain powers regarding church and other
matters. At the time the people of Winchester were allies of Matilda, but after
the Bishop had a disagreement with her he decided to support his brother again,
and went to Winchester; he was determined to persuade the city to change its
allegiance in similar fashion and to besiege her forces in Winchester Castle at
the south-west corner of the city walls. Matilda arrived at Winchester on this
day and the Bishop of Winchester's men retreated behind the walls of Wolvesey
Palace, his residence in the city, fortified in case of attack. He himself escaped,
however, and he rode east to obtain reinforcements from the army of Stephen's
Queen, also named Matilda, near London.

A double siege ensued, with royalists and London
militia blockading the city, while Empress
Matilda besieged the Bishop's men. While
putting Wolvesey under siege, the
Empress set up her headquarters
in the royal castle and Earl Robert
had his at St Swithun's Cathedral.
On 2 August the city was set on
fire, probably by Bishop Henry's
men at Wolvesey. St Mary's
Nunnaminster, Hyde Abbey and
the royal palace were all burnt
to the ground. Empress Matilda
fled in mid-September, helped by
a diversionary attack and skirmish
staged by Robert of Gloucester. Earl
Robert planned an orderly withdrawal
from Winchester, but held back with
his forces to allow her to escape to safety.
Although the citizens had aided the cause of
King Stephen, a small section of the London militia
wrought vengeance, plundering the houses, shops and
churches, and taking many citizens prisoner; many of these prisoners were
tortured and executed on the grounds of having helped the enemy.

The seal of King Stephen. During the twelfth century wars, Winchester found itself under siege for several weeks in 1141.

THOU
SHALT DO NO MURDER

AUGUST

The assassination of the Duke of Buckingham at the
Greyhound Inn, near Portsmouth dockyard,
in August 1628.

1 AUGUST   **1880**   Albert Clark (10) was involved in an altercation with William Mellersh, a boy of about the same age, at Steep, Petersfield. According to Alfred Trigg, one of the witnesses, when the case came to trial at Winchester Assizes on 15 November, Clark came out of church and immediately began throwing stones at Mellersh. The latter asked him not to, and chased him into a barley field. Clark fell down, Mellersh struck him in the face near the right eye, and Clark threatened to cut his head off. He took a knife out of his pocket, and when Mellersh tried to take it away from him Clark stabbed him in the chest. Within an hour he had bled to death.

Clark was arrested and initially charged with wilful murder, but this was later reduced to a charge of manslaughter. The jury found him not guilty, and before discharging him the Hon George Denman, the presiding judge, told him firmly that he must never use a knife again on anybody, no matter how provoked he might be.

2 AUGUST   **1100**   King William II, commonly known as 'William Rufus' because of his mane of red hair, was shot dead while hunting in the New Forest. For a long

The Rufus Stone, in the New Forest, where King William II was reputedly shot in August 1100.

King William II, from a fresco formerly at Rouen Cathedral.

William.

The death of King William II in the New Forest, August 1100, from a nineteenth-century lithograph.

time, tradition had it that the fatal arrow was fired by Walter Tyrrell, a courtier who had been in the hunting party. Tyrrell later swore on oath that he was not in the King's company that day, and never even saw him. Later historians have suggested that the death was no accident, but a carefully planned murder. The King's brother Henry was one of the hunting party, and once he was informed of the King's death he rode at full gallop to Winchester and seized the Treasury. William's body was brought to the city in a charcoal burner's cart next day and hastily buried beneath the cathedral tower. (It fell down seven years later, and the superstitious said it was because the King, who was unmarried and supposed to have certain secret vices, was unworthy of such a holy resting place).

After the burial, Henry held a hastily-convened council at which he was elected his brother's successor as King, and two days later he was crowned King Henry I in Westminster Abbey. Henry was not in fact his elder brother's chosen heir. The man who would otherwise have succeeded him, Robert, was expected to return from his crusade in the Holy Land later in August, bringing a wife with him. Robert, and any son born to him, would therefore displace Henry in the line of royal succession, and only by acting quickly could Henry ensure that the crown would be his. To all outward appearances, it seemed that the King's death was nothing more than an unfortunate accident.

3 AUGUST   1900   Stansted House was destroyed by fire. The owner, Mr George Wilder, had been entertaining a large number of guests during the week, and they left in the morning. At about 8.30 that evening one of the servants discovered flames coming from the roof and raised the alarm. Fire brigades were summoned from Havant and Emsworth, but by then it was realised that the house was doomed. Efforts were made to save the more important articles, including tapestries worth £30,000, pictures, plate and heirlooms, which were carried into the park and placed in charge of the police. Nobody was injured, but the damage was estimated at £200,000, and the house and contents were only insured for £60,000. Mr Wilder had recently been making arrangements to increase the latter sum. Three years later the house was rebuilt on the same site.

4 AUGUST   1852   Isaac Faulkner and Joseph Voke, both of Portsea, were charged by the officer of the revenue cutter *Mermaid* with having a quantity of smuggled spirits on board a small boat. They were remanded for a week.

5 AUGUST   1932   An inquest was held at Micheldever on Francis James Buckley Rutherford (34), a recently retired army officer found early in the morning in his car, on a quiet road near Winchester, with gunshot wounds in his head. Three days earlier he had told his brother Alexander that he had to go to Devonshire very urgently, and that he had 'engaged in some secret job or other – I took it to be secret police, but he did not tell me about it. He said that he had his life in his hands, and if I were to hear something or other that he had been "bumped off" I was not to be surprised.' Alexander told the coroner at the inquest that his brother had never recovered from the effects

of the war. He had gone to serve in France on his eighteenth birthday, had no leave during the first ten months, was wounded twice and very badly gassed. He suffered from a loss of control and temper; he had also had several operations on his nose, and lost his sense of smell, probably as a result of the gas. Later he had difficulty in sleeping, and suffered from violent pain across the eyes. The coroner and jury returned a verdict of 'suicide while of unsound mind', the coroner adding that anyone who had heard his brother's evidence would agree that he was unbalanced, excited and irrational from his war wounds.

Five months earlier, Francis had married the actress Helen Saintsbury. Grief-stricken at his death, and telling friends she could not do without him, in September she shot herself dead in her London flat.

1849 During a severe national outbreak of cholera in the summer, casualties   **6 AUGUST** in Southampton (which had a population of about 32,000) were particularly high. The registrar's returns up to the evening of Friday 10 August showed fifty-seven deaths from the disease, up from thirty-three the previous week, and bringing the total number of deaths to 160 since the first reported case on 3 July. People had petitioned the General Board of Health for the town to be placed under the operation of the Public Health Act, and for a medical inspector to be sent to examine the town. According to the medical correspondent of *The Times*, 'In many parts of Southampton the poor are suffering fearfully, and the notoriously filthy and dangerous state of a great portion of the inferior quarters would seem to render very strong measures indispensable to check the spread of disease in the present juncture, and to prevent pestilence, either in the shape of cholera or fever, from breaking out'.

1913 Mr S.F. Cody, a well-known pioneer airman during the early days of   **7 AUGUST** flight, and Mr W. Evans, of the Sudan Civil Service, were killed in an accident on a trial flight over Cove Common, near Farnborough, an area much used by the Royal Flying Corps, close to the Royal Aircraft factory. They were in a biplane which Cody had built to fly in while competing in the *Daily Mail* seaplane race round Great Britain for a prize of £5,000, due to start on 16 August. It was the second journey which Cody had made that morning, the first one being a mission of seventy miles. A few spectators watched his second, fatal flight. The plane took off shortly after 10 a.m., and was flying steadily at first, until, about half an hour after it had been in the air, the wings were observed to buckle up and the machine fell to the ground. Several members of the Royal Flying Corps were the first to reach the spot, and they found the two men lying dead in the bracken about 60ft from a circular clump of oak trees in which the wreckage was entangled. The machine had torn through the tree branches, but was crumpled up by the resistance of the trunks and was transformed into a shapeless mass of twisted steel rods and wooden spars protruding through the coverings of the large wings. The wreckage was encircled by ropes to keep crowds away – many people had tried to visit, once the news spread – and to allow more detailed examination of the craft by experts who hoped to try and establish the exact cause of the accident.

8 AUGUST

1935 Sisters Betty and Phyllis Oakes were cycling at Winchfield. A car approached and Betty pulled ahead to allow it to pass them safely, but instead the driver deliberately drove so close to them that Phyllis was knocked off and fell onto the bonnet. She was carried thus for about 40yds before she fell off and the car proceeded towards Aldershot without stopping. Two days later she died from her injuries. Meanwhile, two other people had been knocked off their bicycles in similar incidents earlier that week, though neither were fatally injured. The car, which had been stolen at Aldershot, was later found abandoned with minor damage. On the same day that Phyllis Oakes died, another car was stolen in Farnborough, and the driver, Arthur Mortimer (27), was arrested in Guildford after crashing into another vehicle. A Lance-Corporal in the 1st Battalion, Welsh Regiment, stationed at Aldershot, Mortimer was also charged with robbery.

He confessed to several other crimes and appeared at Aldershot Police Court on 30 August, charged with seven offences, including the wilful murder of Phyllis Oakes. Among witnesses for the defence was Mortimer's father, who said his son had been subject to fits after an accident when he was aged twelve. At his trial at Winchester on 25 November the jury found him guilty of murder and he was sentenced to death, but reprieved in February 1936 and detained during His Majesty's pleasure.

9 AUGUST

1934 Four men from Portsmouth Dockyard were admitted to the Royal Naval Hospital, Haslar, suffering from severe burns and shock after a high-tension oil-immersed switch in the motor-generator house in the dockyard burst. A cable short-circuited, almost blinding the men working nearby. Two had severe burns to their face and hands, while the other two had burns on the hands only. First aid was given by members of the crew of the aircraft carrier *Courageous*, one of the ships open to inspection in connection with Portsmouth Navy Week, which had just reported record attendance figures.

10 AUGUST

1938 Acting Pilot Officer R.A. Robertson was piloting one of three aeroplanes from RAF Gosport Station on manoeuvres in Stokes Bay. His plane stalled, fell into the water and sank. A nearby yacht steamed at once to the area, but by then the machine had vanished from sight. His body was recovered in the evening.

11 AUGUST

1910 Madeline Lloyd (26), of Cowes, was committed for trial on three charges of shoplifting at Ryde. She had called at local jewellers' and fancy shops, saying she wanted to collect silver and other articles for presents. In each case, after being shown various articles of jewellery and other goods, she said she would call later with a friend to take the articles – and after she had left the shop, the items chosen had disappeared. When arrested she was carrying a large amount of jewels in a stolen bag. Defending, Mr Thirkell quoted a character reference from a London company which had employed her as housekeeper and gave her an excellent character. Although of humble origins, she was well educated, but had a mania for getting into 'high-class society', which she had been doing lately at the expense of her honesty. She had made a full confession of her thefts, committed out of inordinate vanity, and had not sold any of the items, but given some away as presents. The clerk revealed that she had begun a life of crime nine years earlier, and had been convicted of theft four times already. She was known to the police as something of an expert thief at shops, lodging and private houses. She was admitted to bail, with representatives of her employers being sureties for her for £100 each, and the prisoner entering into her own recognisance of £200.

1882 Francis McDermot, a private in the Black Watch, was charged with assaulting Constable Holbrook. Early in the morning the policeman heard the sound of smashing glass, and on going to the Still Cavern, Kent Street, saw McDermot at the window. He asked the soldier 'what he was about', whereupon McDermot ran away. The officer blew his whistle, and two other officers appeared on the scene. When McDermot saw them he turned round and struck Holbrook a violent blow, which completely closed the right eye. He was fined 20s, or five days' imprisonment.
12 AUGUST

1927 An inquest was held at Sandown on the body of Albert Edward Dellow, a Hampshire man who had run amok earlier that week. He had a wife at Portsmouth but was separated from her, and he had lived with a woman and her daughter for several years. One day he attacked them both with a sword, and both needed treatment in hospital. He then wrote them a letter, saying, 'All regrets are too late now and I am taking the only way out, for the devils are still prompting me to kill, and placing weapons in my hands.' He threw himself over the cliffs and suffered fatal injuries. The sword was picked up about a mile away from the house. A verdict of suicide while of unsound mind was returned.
13 AUGUST

Sandown in about 1920, where Albert Dellow killed himself after attacking his common-law wife and her daughter in 1927.

1829 An accident occurred on the river Test near Netley Fort. A party consisting of Mr Missing, a linen draper, Mr Baker, a grocer, Mr Pegler, a silversmith, and his son, and a Mr Brown had been to Cowes regatta and were returning in *Red Rover*, Pegler's pleasure boat, under a heavy press of canvas, when a squall upset the boat. All were thrown into the water, but the elder Mr Pegler and Brown were picked up in an exhausted state by some of a yacht crew who had seen the mishap. They were the only lucky ones, for by this time the bodies of the others had disappeared below the surface, and none were recovered. Mr Missing (20) was the eldest of a large orphan family who relied largely on the success of his drapery business for financial support. Baker (23) was his cousin and one of his father's executors, and his recently-established grocery business had been showing every sign of success. In reporting the tragedy, the *Hampshire Advertiser* noted that they hoped it would 'act as a caution, and put an end to the foolish practice here with young men (who think themselves clever, and would have
14 AUGUST

others think them so too), attempting the management of their boats in a river which, from its locality, is always subject to squalls of wind... a day's excursion in a boat should not be considered a day's pleasure without a waterman being on board'.

15 AUGUST   **1924**   The body of Mrs Lucy Fisher, the wife of a leather finisher, was found in a cornfield between Basingstoke and the village of Sherborne St John. She had been hacked to death, her eyes kicked out, her skull fractured and she had been sexually assaulted. Two days earlier she had been seen walking in that direction with William Matthews (24), and later that night he went home in a distressed condition, telling his sister Edith he had killed a woman. On being questioned, he said that Mrs Fisher had been 'jawing' him about money, that she caught hold of his neck, and he could remember no more. Lucy's widower, Charles, said that she often went out in the evenings, but seemed totally unaware of her involvement with another man. Letters found in Matthews's room proved that she had been having an affair with him and seeing him regularly in the few weeks before her death.

He went on trial on 24 November. As a witness, his sister told the court that he had suffered from ill-health since he was a small boy, and had served in the army but been discharged as unfit; he was suffering from neurasthenia. Since then he had worked as a waiter, footman, trouser-presser and pianist. He had also been briefly in the Royal Marines, but was discharged on medical grounds and sent home in the care of a marine. Since then he had been in hospital with paralysis and epilepsy, was once found with his head in a gas oven, and was afraid to sleep in the dark. On another occasion he broke all the crockery in his room, and he was often irritable without any apparent reason.

Dr East stated that he had examined the prisoner and found him nervous, apprehensive and suicidal, having attempted to kill himself while in prison. At the time of the offence, he said, Matthews probably did not know what he was doing, or that what he did was wrong. Without needing to retire, the jury returned a unanimous verdict of guilty but insane, and the judge, Mr Justice Greer, ordered that he should be detained during His Majesty's pleasure.

16 AUGUST   **1849**   Mr T. Dann, a plumber at Ryde, was working on a well at St Peter's. He descended using a rope and it was thought that he was affected by the foul air. In letting go he fell between 60 and 70ft, and was killed after being badly mutilated by coming into contact with the sides of the well.

17 AUGUST   **1888**   Charles Andrews of Forton promised to sign the pledge and was bound over to keep the peace for one month. On 15 August, he had been charged at Gosport Police Court with assaulting his wife. Three days earlier he came home the worse for drink, quarrelled with his wife, caught hold of her wrist, dragged her into the sitting room, and struck her on the forehead. She hit him in return and he retaliated in kind several times.

18 AUGUST   **1952**   John Alcott, a railway fireman at Eltham, planned to go with his wife to France on holiday. He told her he was going to collect his outstanding holiday pay, and would be back within two or three hours. However, he actually had other plans, which included taking a train to Aldershot, where he bought a sheath knife and spent the night in a hotel. On 20 August he enquired about trains from Aldershot station, and two days later the booking clerk, Geoffrey Dean, was found stabbed to death in the booking office; £169 in cash was missing and empty bags which should have contained cash were strewn around the floor. Abbott was arrested at his lodgings on 23 August, confessed to the murder, and told police that they would find the murder weapon up the chimney. He appeared before magistrates at Farnborough, and was tried at Kingston-on-Thames in November. The defence tried to argue that he was insane at the time of the killing, but the jury found him guilty, an appeal was dismissed and he was executed at Wandsworth on 2 January 1953.

1954   Michael Fell (14), of River View Cottage, Alton, was found dead at home after experimenting with a baby's gas mask which he had attached to a gas cooker.   **19 AUGUST**

1899   Reuben Leavey (18), a hawker, in company with William Nutbean (17) and George Clark (19), both labourers, robbed John Chambers of a watch and chain, food and 16s in cash in Southampton, threatening him with violence if he did not comply. They were arrested and charged at Winchester Assizes on 4 November, but as the only witness against the prisoners did not appear a formal verdict of 'not guilty' was accepted, and they were discharged.   **20 AUGUST**

1887   Harriet Smith (59) was charged at Gosport Police Court and remanded to Portsmouth, accused of unlawfully wounding her husband with intent to do him grievous bodily harm. In the course of an argument she took a razor and inflicted a severe wound in her husband's face. When charged, she said, 'I was cutting my corns with a razor, and he aggravated me so that I cut at him.' Superintendent Catchlove said that if she had cut him in the throat, she might have caused his death. 'Yes,' she replied, 'I should have been transported for life, and then I should have been a happy woman.'   **21 AUGUST**

1954   A calf was drowned in a field at Oakhanger Farm, near Bordon, during a thunderstorm and torrential rain over north-east Hampshire. Traffic also had to be diverted when a road between East Tisted and Farringdon vanished under 2ft of water, and one street in Selborne had water 3ft deep.   **22 AUGUST**

1628   George Villiers, 1st Duke of Buckingham, was assassinated at Portsmouth. He had been a favourite of Kings James I and Charles I, and made many enemies in the process, especially after the disastrous failure of his military expeditions to Spain and then France. In the summer of 1628 he went to Portsmouth to organise a second campaign against the French, and established his headquarters at the Greyhound Inn, near the dockyard. On this day he went into the hall of the inn, and while talking to one of his colonels he was stabbed in the chest. He died almost at once.   **23 AUGUST**

The assassination of George Villiers, Duke of Buckingham, at Portsmouth in August 1628.

The assassin, John Felton, a Lieutenant in the army, escaped in the confusion but then gave himself up. He had been wounded in the first French onslaught the previous year, and believed the Duke had denied him advancement as well as withholding some of his pay. While reading the remonstrance from the House of Parliament, a formal statement by the Commons asking the King to consider dismissing Buckingham from his offices, Felton became convinced that 'by killing the Duke he should do his country great service'. He was arrested, taken before the magistrates, and sent to the Tower of London. The privy council wanted to have him questioned while under torture on the

Felton, the Duke's assassin, in the dungeons of the Tower.

rack, but they were overruled by the judges, who declared that to do so would be contrary to English law. Nevertheless, he was tried by the King's Bench on 27 November, pleaded guilty, and hanged at Tyburn the next day. His body was sent back to Portsmouth in chains to be publicly exhibited as 'a lesson in disgrace', but the people regarded him as something of a martyr.

[There is some dispute about the dates. Some sources say the assassination was in April, with the trial and execution following in October].

1867 Three little girls from Alton, Fanny Adams and Lizzie Warner (both 8) and Fanny's younger sister Lizzie, went out to play in Flood Meadow nearby. On their way they met Frederick Baker (29), a clerk who worked in the town office of Clements Solicitors. He joined them in their games for a while, helped them to pick berries, and then gave Minnie and Lizzie some money, telling them to buy themselves sweets and then go back home. When they had gone he offered Fanny more money if she would walk with him; she took it, but then burst into tears, deciding she wanted to go home as well. He picked her up and took her with him. When she failed to return home by the evening a search was mounted for her, and one of the party found the severed head of a child between two hop poles. A further look revealed several more dismembered body parts.

24 AUGUST

Baker had been pointed out to a neighbour by Lizzie while he was coming out of a gate near the meadow, and she said he was the man who had given them the money. As he looked quite respectable, and appeared calm enough, he was not immediately suspected, but after the gruesome discoveries a policeman went to Clements' office and arrested him in connection with the murder. He was charged the next day, and a diary was found in his office in which the previous day's entry read: 'Killed a young girl. It was fine and hot'. Dr Louis Leslie, who carried out the post-mortem, came to the conclusion that Fanny had been

Fanny Adams, murdered at Flood Meadow, Alton, on 24 August 1867. *(Illustrated Police News)*

An artist's impression of the abduction and murder of Fanny Adams in August 1867. *(Illustrated Police News)*

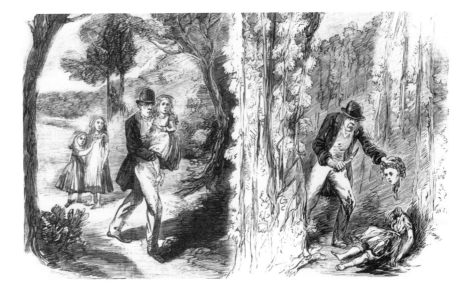

The execution of Frederick Baker, Fanny Adams's murderer, at Winchester in December 1867. He was the last person to be hanged in public in Hampshire. *(Illustrated Police News)*

hit on the top of the head with a large stone. One was found in the hop fields nearby, with traces of blood and hair, and the person who found it took it home to display on his windowsill.

The two-day trial of Baker opened at Winchester Assizes on 5 December. He appeared to have been a cultured, well-educated man who had turned to drinking heavily after a broken engagement, and was suspected of having murdered a small girl in Surrey, a crime for which another man was hanged despite protesting his innocence. Doctors gave evidence of insanity in the family, but the jury found him guilty without making a recommendation to mercy. On 24 December, he became the last person to be publicly hanged at Winchester.

25 AUGUST

1932 John Illingworth (31), a leading stoker aboard HMS *Dolphin*, Portsmouth, and Rose Cooper (27), a married woman, of Brading, Isle of Wight, were charged on remand at Lambeth with attempting to commit suicide by inhaling coal gas. They had arrived in London on 6 August and taken a room at a house in

Brook Street, Kennington. On 13 August they were found lying on a bed, unconscious, given first aid and taken to Lambeth Hospital for treatment for gas poisoning. In the room the police found a letter from Illingworth, saying that they had both arranged 'this affair' before they left Portsmouth, and they wished to be buried together. Mrs Cooper's husband, a naval pensioner, had been seen by the local police, but refused to have anything more to do with her and had declined to come to London. An officer serving on board the *Dolphin* stated that Illingworth had been in the Service since 1918, was of good character, and would not be recommended for discharge in consequence of these proceedings.

Illingworth was bound over in his own recognisances in £10 to come up for judgment if called upon within three years, and Cooper was sentenced to two months' imprisonment with hard labour.

1888   Thomas Jones, an army pensioner who worked as a barber at St Mary   **26 AUGUST**
Street, Portsmouth, killed his wife Eliza and then himself. They had married in 1885, but she was 'a woman of ill repute and dissolute habits'. They had lived together on reasonably good terms until about three months earlier, when they quarrelled as a result of her infidelity and separated. She went to live with an artilleryman, and on 8 August they met accidentally at Landport. He asked her to come back to him, but she refused, and he struck her, threatening to kill her. For this he appeared before the magistrates and was bound over in his own recognisances to keep the peace for a month. On the night of 25 August she went to the Naval and Military Arms, Portsmouth, with a female companion. She left at about 10.30 p.m., very drunk, saying she was going to her husband's house to collect some clothing. They were heard quarrelling at around midnight, though the neighbours were so used to it that they thought nothing of it. On the next day his customers were surprised to find his shop closed. By afternoon the neighbours were increasingly suspicious. They called the police, who forced an entry into the premises and found the bodies of husband and wife with their throats cut. Examination suggested that there had been a struggle, that he had taken her life and then his own.

1817   The *Morning Chronicle* reported: 'A few days since, Mr Cooper, a brewer in   **27 AUGUST**
this town [Ryde], put a period to his existence, by drowning himself in a vessel of his own beer in his brewhouse. He had told his family he was going to Earl Spencer's. After being absent from his home for some time, inquiry was made at the Noble Earl's, and it was ascertained that he had not been there. Search was then made in the brewhouse, when he was discovered by his hat, and one of his hands seen above the beer. He must have used considerable exertion to force himself into the vessel, as it was rather less than his body. A low desponding state of mind is assigned as the cause of the rash act. He has left a widow and a numerous family to lament his loss.'

1931   Madge Cleife (15), a factory hand at Portsmouth Steel Co., left her home   **28 AUGUST**
in the town after supper, and when she did not return later that night her father reported her as missing. She was found dead beside a footpath on the golf course

at Great Salterns, Portsmouth, by two schoolboys on the next day, having been strangled with the belt of her raincoat. William Kell (19), with whom she was known to have been on friendly terms, admitted having been with her that evening. After being interviewed by police he was arrested on a charge of murder. He went on trial at Winchester Assizes in November but was found not guilty. Nobody else was arrested in connection with the murder, which was never solved.

29 AUGUST   **1782**   HMS *Royal George*, the largest warship in the world at the time of her launch in 1756, sank off Portsmouth while preparing to sail with a fleet commanded by Admiral Richard Howe to Gibraltar. She was being heeled over at an angle to allow for minor repairs to be made. A supply vessel approached her on her low side to transfer a cargo of rum, and the extra weight, together with that of the crewmen unloading the cargo, caused the ship to heel so much that the sea washed in at her gun ports and she soon began to ship water in her hold. A breeze on the raised side forced her further over: water rushed in, she rolled over on her side and sank before any distress signal could be given. About 900 people, including 300 women and 60 children visiting the ship in harbour, as well as Captain Richard Kempenfelt, were drowned. Around 230 survived, some by running up the rigging, while others were picked up by boats from other vessels. Most of the dead were washed ashore at Ryde and were buried together in a mass grave. A court-martial exonerated the officers and crew, many of whom were among the dead, and attributed the accident to the general state of decay of her timbers.

30 AUGUST   **1920**   Private Squire of the King's Royal Rifle Corps was committed on a charge of bigamy at Hampshire Assizes. Ellen Tingley said she met him in April at Eastbourne, where he was an inmate of Summerdown Military Convalescent Camp. They were married on 21 August at Farnham. Four days later she went to Aldershot Barracks and met the first Mrs Squire, who had married him in April 1919. 'He had always been one of the best of men,' said the latter.

31 AUGUST   **1888**   Edward Keen (24), a drum major in the Portsmouth division of the Royal Marine Light Infantry, was charged on remand at Gosport Police Court with committing acts of gross indecency at Forton Barracks on 13 and 19 August. For the prosecution, Richard Parkins (16) said that the prisoner took him to his bedroom on the first date and committed an offence. Six days later he asked him to come to his room again, but Parkins refused and made a complaint to Corporal Scotney, NCO in charge of the barrack room occupied by the drummer boys. Another boy also made a similar complaint. Scotney reported it to Bugle-Major Bond, who questioned Parkins, as a result of which Keen was arrested and handed over to the police. For the defence, Mr Feltham said that the case against the prisoner was not fully substantiated, and Parkin's statement was not corroborated. The prosecution had provided no medical testimony, and the prisoner was therefore discharged.

SEPTEMBER

Badajos Barracks, Aldershot, where James Ellis served and from where he went missing in 1923.
(© *Nicola Sly*)

1 SEPTEMBER   **1871**   Mary Anne Maude (29), a widow living in West End Street, Southampton, died from severe burns. On 29 August, at about 2.15 a.m., she had been asleep in bed – while her sister, Emily Payne (14), and brother, Philip (7) – slept on the floor in the same room, when a fire broke out. They had all retired soon after midnight, and she left a candle alight beside her bed. When Emily woke she found the bed on fire; she did her best to put the flames out and raised the alarm. A neighbour came to her assistance, and they moved her to the front room. Dr Cheesman was called to look after her and arranged for her to be moved to the local infirmary, but her injuries were so severe that she only lived another three days. All the bedclothes had been destroyed.

2 SEPTEMBER   **1685**   Alice Lisle was executed in Winchester market place. After the battle of Sedgemoor (*see* 6 July 1685 above), she gave refuge at her home, Moyles Court, near Ringwood, to two fugitives from the Duke of Monmouth's defeated army. John Hickes, a non-conformist minister, and his associate, Richard Nelthorpe, both outlawed and under sentence of death, asked her for shelter in mid-July, and she agreed to take them in. They were arrested the following morning, and she was charged with harbouring traitors. She went on trial in front of Judge Jeffreys at the opening of the Bloody Assizes in Winchester and pleaded that not only did she have no sympathy with the rebellion, but that she did not know Hickes was guilty of anything other than illegal preaching. The jury had some sympathy with her, but they were directed to find her guilty of being an accessory

The arrest of Alice Lisle in September 1685. She had given refuge to two fugitives from the Duke of Monmouth's army at her home near Ringwood.

to traitors against the King. She was sentenced to be burned at the stake that same afternoon, but Jeffreys granted her a few days' respite, and the King allowed her to be beheaded instead of burnt.

A plaque opposite the Eclipse Inn near Winchester Cathedral marks the site of her execution. She was buried in a tomb on the right-hand side of the porch at St Mary's Church, Ellingham. According to local folklore, her headless ghost is said to haunt the lanes around Moyles Court, now a school, and rattles along the road from the Court to St Mary's Church in a coach drawn by four headless horses.

3 SEPTEMBER   **1930**   An inquest was held at Portsmouth on the body of Lilina May Nichols (34), of College Street, Portsea, who had died suddenly on 16 August. She had been living with William Stonehouse (39), a stoker serving in HMS *Centurion*. At the time of her death she had injuries to her face, which she told neighbours earlier had been caused by a soldier who struck her with a whip. Statements were produced which alleged that Stonehouse (a sailor, not a soldier) had assaulted her. He was warned that he would have to attend a coroner's inquiry into her death, but on 26 August he hanged himself on board his ship. The police surgeon, Dr Hamer Hodges, told the jury that Nichols died from haemorrhage of the brain, probably caused by her injuries, but might have perished from natural causes, and the jury returned an open verdict. An inquest was then

held on the body of Stonehouse, and a verdict of suicide while of unsound mind was recorded.

1868 A major fire raged for several hours in Southampton Docks, resulting in the destruction of the most valuable part of the Royal Mail's Company Factory and a portion of the building and engine room of the adjoining sugar house. It had started in the carpenter's shop of the factory and spread quickly. Nobody was injured, but losses included the engineer's library and much valuable machinery.

4 SEPTEMBER

1910 Lieutenant Siegfried Helm (23), of the 21st Battalion Nassau Regiment, was observed by two British officers, Captain Martelli and Lieutenant Salmon, while they were riding on Portsdown Hills. They had seen him taking measurements and notes while standing close to the wire fencing around Widley Fort. When he saw he was being watched, he stopped his work and walked away. They approached him and asked him for his card and notebook. He was detained at Fort Purbrook, Cosham, and charged with being outside certain fortresses belonging to the King, among them Fort Southsea Castle, Portsmouth Harbour, Fort Purbrook and Farlington Redoubt. At all of them he had made sketches and taken notes without authority, apparently for the purpose of communicating them to a foreign state, namely the German empire. When arrested, he said that he had come to England in August for a few weeks' holiday.

5 SEPTEMBER

He went on trial at Winchester Assizes before Mr Justice Bankes on 14 November, where he pleaded guilty, expressed his profound and sincere regret at violating the laws of the country whose hospitality he was enjoying, and gave an undertaking never to do such a thing again. He was bound over in the sum of £250 and discharged.

1808 A young man discovered the body of a soldier, covered in blood, in a lane near Lymington Barracks belonging to the German depot. The dead man, Corporal Dan Bamback, had been seen a short while previously in the company of 'a German woman of loose character', with a sergeant from the same regiment, John Mass, of the Chasseurs Britanniques, following them at a fairly

6 SEPTEMBER

Lymington High Street, *c.* 1960. Corporal Dan Bamback was stabbed to death at the old barracks nearby in September 1808.

fast pace. The full contingent of soldiers was ordered on parade, and Mass was conspicuous by his absence. It emerged he had been jealous of the corporal and had stabbed him to death. After the inquest he was charged with wilful murder, and taken into custody to stand trial at the next assizes.

7 SEPTEMBER **1893** Another military tragedy was revealed, this time at Winchester, with an inquest at the Barracks Hospital into the death of Lance-Corporal James Stanley Gardner (27), of the King's Royal Rifles. At about 8.45 a.m. the previous morning Private Charles Lemon, of the same regiment, went on parade. Less than an hour later he returned to find Gardner, who had been sitting in his room, lying on the floor dying from a shotgun wound in his chest. The bullet had gone through his body, belt, haversack and wooden water bottle (which had been hanging on the wall), and embedded itself in the brickwork. Gardner had been acting rather strangely for about three weeks, and earlier that morning Lemon asked him if he knew that he had been reported as absent again at parade. His answer was that he realised, but would sooner die than appear on parade again. On the bed was a letter to his wife, dated 29 August, saying that 'as everything seems to go against me, I think I am better out of the way'. It was said at the hearing that he had money worries, and there was apparently nothing with regard to his regimental duties to worry him. A verdict of suicide while of unsound mind was recorded.

8 SEPTEMBER **1868** Henry Barnes (23), a carter employed by Mr Middleton, was killed while working in the latter's quarry at Shanklin. James Jeffery, a labourer, told the inquest at the Crab Inn on 10 September that he had been digging stone for nearly an hour when Barnes came in his horse and cart to remove some. The loose stone was about 12ft from the top of the quarry and had been undermined about 4ft. Barnes gave it six blows with a sledgehammer, and Jeffery then warned him to come away at once, as he could see it was about to fall.

Disregarding him, Barnes administered a seventh blow, and a large block of stone, weighing at least six tons, was immediately dislodged. Barnes tried to run away, but in doing so stepped on a stone which rolled and threw him on the ground. The large block caught him by the heel, and another block fell on his head, killing him instantly. Jeffery and another man fetched a couple of iron bars and rolled the stone off his body within two minutes, but it was evident that he never had a chance of survival.

Shanklin undercliff, near the quarry where
Henry Barnes was accidentally killed in
September 1868.

1871 John Feaney allegedly attacked Martha Wyett, a children's nurse, at Millbrook, Southampton. When he appeared at Winchester Assizes on 13 December, Wyett told the Court she was taking her charges out in a perambulator when he jumped out of the hedge, raped her, and threatened to choke her if she resisted; he then offered her *2s* to say nothing about it to anybody else. She refused his money and told Mrs Gulliver, her employer. When questioned by the defence, she denied that she had been 'imprudent' with other men. Nevertheless, Feaney was found not guilty and acquitted. **9 SEPTEMBER**

1961 Helen Johnson, wife of a naval rating and mother of two small children, was found strangled in bed in her flat at Portsea. Leonard Askham (22) of Harlow, a naval engineer mechanic serving on board HMS *Hermes*, was charged with killing her. At his trial at Winchester Assizes on 8 December he was found guilty of manslaughter and sentenced to three years' imprisonment. **10 SEPTEMBER**

1871 James Leak, a fireman with the Peninsular & Oriental Co., came back to his home at Portswood in the evening, very drunk. After sleeping on the sofa, he went out again next morning, returned about 3 p.m. to collect some possessions and left a second time, then returned about 7 p.m. with his stepson. Both were very much the worse for drink, and he quarrelled with his wife, Ann. A poker was lying nearby, and her daughter picked it up to try and stop him from using it against his wife. As he seized it from her he fell over backwards, and the poker hit his wife, going part of the way into her breast. At Winchester Assizes on 13 December he pleaded that it had been an accident. His wife agreed that he had not intended to stab her, telling the court that he had always been a good husband, but his son had led him into drunkenness and bad ways. The judge considered it a case of unlawful wounding and the jury agreed, while recommending him to mercy. He was given one month's imprisonment. **11 SEPTEMBER**

1874 Captain John Bird was shot dead at Aldershot Barracks. On the previous day, Thomas Smith, of the 20th Hussars, had been sentenced to seven days' confinement to barracks for falling out of ranks without permission. He took his revenge by killing Bird at target practice, and as he was led away to the guard room, he muttered, 'He would give no more seven days' drill, and it would be a warning to others'. After being tried at Winchester Assizes and found guilty of murder, he wrote a voluntary confession in which he admitted that 'nothing can justify the dreadful sin I committed'. He was hanged on 16 November. **12 SEPTEMBER**

1863 Mr Drake, employed by Mr Ransom of Southampton, was driving through Romsey on a heavily laden timber wagon. He and two other men had been to Standbridge, two miles away, to collect some timber. They stopped at several pubs on their return journey. By the time he reached Latimer Street, Drake was very tipsy. As the cart passed through the tollgate on Southampton Road, he lost his balance and slipped off. The wheel ran over him in a slanting direction, he was picked up and taken to a small outhouse attached to the toll gate, but was already dead. An inquest the next day recorded a verdict of accidental death, 'accelerated being at the time in a state of intoxication'. **13 SEPTEMBER**

14 SEPTEMBER **1928**   Josephine (Molly) West (17) was charged at Portsmouth Police Court with aiding and abetting Mrs Lilian Wallis to abandon a child at Portsmouth on 14 August. Detective Sergeant Mardlen stated in evidence that she was brought up on this charge on 20 August and remanded for a week. She escaped from the police matron while being taken to Winchester Gaol, but was recaptured on 12 September and arrested in London. While being held in the police cells she tried to kill herself but only inflicted a slight wound on her wrist. She said that if she was sent to a home she would 'lead them a tidy dance'. The previous year she had been sent to a convent in Bristol, from which she escaped.

She was remanded until 17 September, when she appeared in court again. Her mother pleaded with the Bench to let the girl go home where she could look after her. When questioned as to her own past, Mrs West said she had been deprived of a pension granted to her after her husband, an army corporal, was killed in the war. She had lost the pension through 'being led away and becoming addicted to drink'. The Bench bound Josephine over within £20 for three years, and ordered her to be placed under the probation officer at Clerkenwell for that period.

15 SEPTEMBER **1880**   Louisa Godding (aged 30 months) was deliberately drowned at Gosport. The infant's mother Fanny (39), from Alverstoke, had been a servant at the Pier Hotel, Southsea, and brought her daughter to a Mrs Allen at Portsea to look after. Louisa had been very sickly at the time, but her state of health soon improved. At about 7 a.m. Mrs Godding visited Mrs Allen to ask for the child. Mrs Allen asked her to wait for a few minutes, and went out. When she returned, she find mother and child had both gone, and informed the police. Meanwhile several other people had seen them, 'apparently in a state of trouble'. At about 10 p.m., Mrs Godding was found by a policeman in the water in a creek of Portsmouth

Alverstoke, home of Fanny Godding, whose infant daughter was drowned in September 1880. (© *Diane Webb*)

Harbour. She confessed she had been trying to kill herself, was taken to the police station, and recognised as the woman who had taken the child from Mrs Allen's house. When asked where the child was, she admitted, after some hesitation, that she had drowned it at Gosport by holding it under water until it was dead, and told the police where the body could be found.

The body was found in the mud next morning. Mrs Godding said that she had already decided for some time that she meant to do away with herself, but if she did, Mrs Allen would send the child back to her father, and she knew she could not afford to keep it, so she decided to drown it instead. She was tried at Winchester Assizes on 17 November, and the defence counsel contended that she was insane. She had had to give up her job because of illness; she had suffered from erysipelas in the head, and frequent attacks of delirium. There was no evidence of any intention to kill the child. The jury took only twenty minutes to reach a verdict of not guilty on the grounds of insanity, and Mr Justice Denman ordered her to be detained during Her Majesty's pleasure.

1890   Henry Turner (20), Daniel McCarthy (20), and Herbert Benyon (26),   16 SEPTEMBER
three soldiers from the King's Royal Rifle Corps, took advantage of a benefactor and ended up in court. Arthur Fullick, a labourer, went into a public house at Aldershot, entered into conversation with the three men and bought them each a drink. They then got up to leave, but McCarthy persuaded Fullick to accompany them. A constable was outside watching the premises in case it was necessary to report the landlord for permitting drunkenness on the premises. He saw the four men go up the hill together. Once they were out of sight – or so they thought – the soldiers attacked Fullick and stole four sovereigns from his pocket. Fortunately for him, however, a cyclist rode by at that moment, and went straight to the police station to tell them what he had seen. The soldiers were caught and identified by the victim. They appeared at Winchester Assizes on 11 December. Benyon was acquitted, but the other two were sentenced to twelve months' imprisonment with hard labour.

1823   John Rattu (17) accidentally shot his brother William dead in their   17 SEPTEMBER
grounds at Fratton. Their father Richard was angry about their gardens being regularly plundered, so he sent John and another youth to keep watch during the night. He gave John a gun and ordered him to fire if anybody else appeared on the premises. At about 1.30 a.m., John, having heard a noise among the fruit trees, came to his father in some distress and said he had shot William. The boy was taken home, but died two days later. Mr Rattu said to his wounded son, 'That is what you get by keeping company with rascals'. John appeared at Winchester Assizes in March 1824. Although he had acted under his father's direction, Mr Sergeant Bosanquet told him that he had committed an illegal act, and he felt it his duty to pass a more severe sentence than he might otherwise have done, in the hope that it would be a warning to others not to resort to such illegal methods for the protection of their property. He was imprisoned in a house of correction for six months.

18 SEPTEMBER 1878   Mrs Cameron, widow of Lieutenant-General Cameron, director of the Ordnance Survey, who had died in July, died by her own hand at Southampton. According to reports in the papers, she had 'for some little time suffered from an aberration of intellect accelerated by grief, which had assumed the character of religious mania, but although her state had been very weak and depressed, no serious fears were entertained of her intention to terminate her life'. She was in her bedroom in the morning, and did not reply when she was called. Servants forced the door, and found her with her throat cut, grasping a razor tightly in her hand. A doctor was called at once, but she was already dead.

19 SEPTEMBER 1863   Ann Vender (36), who was notorious in the Landport area for her dissolute habits, died a few days after being taken to the local police station while 'drunk and incapable'. She was badly bruised after having fallen down several times while 'in a state of helpless inebriety'. She was taken ill at home, and died from lockjaw, a verdict confirmed at an inquest at the Jordan Inn, Chandos Street, Landport.

20 SEPTEMBER 1954   Michael Tragett (28), a schoolmaster at Awbridge Danes School, Romsey, was charged at Hampshire Quarter Sessions after a case which followed a clash between village boys and pupils from the school on 10 July, in which one youth was ducked in a lake. He pleaded not guilty but was convicted of assaulting Peter Bacon (17) and occasioning him actual bodily harm, and of a common assault on Neville James (16). Bacon said in court that he and nine companions were turned back by Tragett from walking along a footpath on the edge of the Tragett's estate. Tragett told them they were trespassing and Bacon replied that he thought it was a public footpath, whereupon the schoolmaster took him by the shoulders and tried to trip him; in response, he tried to tread on Tragett's feet. Then the village boys returned with Constable George. Tragett suggested throwing them all into the lake, and James was pushed in the water. Tragett said that the constable swore at him while the village boys were 'screaming their heads off'. Some of his pupils wanted to dip the villagers in the lake, but Mrs Tragett, the master's mother, said, 'Certainly not'. Tragett said he went down to the lake to see that nobody was drowned, and had hold of James's leg when he was dipped in the lake.

Mrs Tragett, who admitted suggesting that they dipped one of the village youths in the lake to stop them from using bad language, was cleared of all charges and discharged, but her son was sentenced to six months' imprisonment and ordered to pay £30 towards the cost of the prosecution.

1872 Mr Bernard, a young barrister, was drowned in a squall during stormy weather in Southampton Waters. The only child of Mr Joseph Bernard, a well-liked and much respected borough and county magistrate in the city, he had only recently been called to the bar, and had just held his first brief at the recent Winchester Assizes. He was said to have had a promising career in front of him.

1886 William Smith (44), a painter, of Southsea, deliberately threw himself from the steam launch *Frances* in Portsmouth Harbour. He was rescued and handed over to a constable, who remanded him in custody for attempting suicide.

Portsmouth Harbour and Portchester. William Smith tried to drown himself here in September 1886. (*Hampshire Telegraph & Naval Chronicle*)

1923 The dismembered remains of James Ellis (21), serving with the 1st Battalion of the Leicestershire Regiment at Badajos Barracks, Aldershot were found under gorse bushes in the Long Valley, about half a mile away. He had been absent without leave since 23 May. One of the first men to be interviewed during police enquiries was his friend, Lance-Corporal Albert Dearnley (20), who made a confession saying that on a walk together Ellis had produced a rope and suggested they have a game of cowboys and Indians. Dearnley had bound and gagged Ellis, who had vowed he would wriggle free without any trouble. Dearnley took him at his word, pushed him under some gorse bushes, and returned to camp. That night he overslept, and Ellis failed to return to camp – for obvious reasons.

At the inquest the jury returned a verdict of wilful murder, and Dearnley went on trial at Winchester Assizes on 27 November. Two other men from the battalion gave evidence that they had seen both prisoner and victim leaving the barracks together the night the latter disappeared. It seemed that they had had a strange relationship, appearing the best of friends at one moment and then fighting the next, with a bleeding Dearnley commenting after one such occasion that he would 'have [Ellis] again sooner or later'. The counsel for the defence said that Dearnley had not intended to commit murder, and while they could not say he was legally insane, they thought him incapable of appreciating the consequences of his actions. After a one-day trial, Mr Justice Avory sentenced him to death. Dearnley was due to be executed on 8 January 1924, but he lodged an appeal, and information came to light suggesting that the death was not due to murder but an accident that had occurred in the course of a homosexual ritual between both men. Dearnley, who was engaged to be married, feared that Ellis would reveal the nature of their relationship to his fiancée Hilda Storey, and this was apparently his way of silencing him. On 11 January the sentence was commuted to life imprisonment.

24 SEPTEMBER 1932   Albert Joiner (51), a signalman, was working the signals in the station box at Fareham when he suddenly felt unwell. He telephoned to the stationmaster to ask if he could be relieved. Another man was sent to take over, but only just arrived in the box to take over when Joiner collapsed and died.

25 SEPTEMBER 1905   For several weeks around this time, Basingstoke was in the grip of an epidemic of enteric fever, or typhoid. During the second half of July, an investigation had been carried out into the state of the town's drains, and pipes were inserted to stop the flow of sewage. An overflow at one point was reported at the end of August, and later it was found that the contents of an obstructed drain had contaminated a well which was part of the water supply. On 18 September, two cases were noticed in the borough; four more were counted two days later, six a day after that, with fifteen, sixteen and twenty-two respectively on the next three days. By 11 October the total had reached 147, with seven deaths reported.

Basingstoke, Winchester Street, *c.* 1900. The town was severely affected by an outbreak of typhoid fever in September 1905.

Lower Church Street and St Michael's Church, Basingstoke, *c.* 1900.

The population of Basingstoke was estimated at between 9,000 and 10,000, and the health authorities feared that at least 1.5 per cent of people were affected. For a while the town was shunned by people from other surrounding communities. On 23 October, the press suggested that the Mayor should have acted more quickly and tried to allay the general alarm which had ensued as a result of the epidemic. He was reported 'to have expressed his hope that the people in the district would be reassured that they could come to Basingstoke without the slightest danger of taking the fever, which was not in the air at all.'

1859 A violent storm swept over the town and neighbourhood of Southampton during the afternoon, flooding several homes and cellars in the lower part of town. Rainfall of 2.05in was recorded between 2.15 and 4.30 p.m., but there was no sign of any thunder or lightning.

26 SEPTEMBER

1886 George Enfield, a hawker, was summoned at Portsmouth Police Court for having assaulted Edward Garnett on 18 September, knocking his teeth out and giving him two black eyes. The complainant alleged that Enfield had met him that night, and without any provocation hit out at him. Enfield alleged that Garnett had entered his house and insulted him, afterwards repeating his conduct in the street. The magistrates said the charge was a serious one, and sentenced Enfield to one month's hard labour.

27 SEPTEMBER

1859 Constable Todd was on duty on Gosport beach shortly before midnight when James Sharlin, of the 86th Regiment, approached him saying he had been robbed of £5. With him was a friend, George Wilson, a recruit in the Hampshire Artillery. Sharlin said he had lost the money in the Three Guns Inn nearby, and asked Todd if he would go and make enquiries of anybody who was still there. The policeman did so, but found neither the money nor anybody to question. When he came out to report his failure, Wilson said angrily, 'as you have not found money we will give it to you', and began beating him with his belt. Egged on, Sharlin joined in the attack, striking Todd with his bare fists. Wilson was fined 5gns plus costs, and in default of payment, he was committed for two months' hard labour, while Sharlin was discharged on entering into his own recognisances of £5 to keep the peace for a month.

28 SEPTEMBER

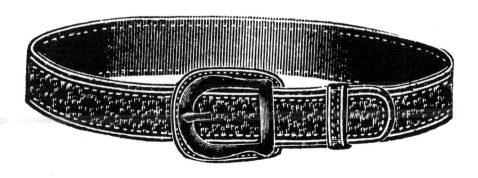

29 SEPTEMBER   **1873**   Alice Roe, a maidservant aged about 15, had been left in charge of James Williams (3), of Granada Road, Southsea. At about 8 a.m. she heard him in his room, crying fretfully. She ran upstairs to find out why, and found him sitting up in bed with his nightdress and some of his bedclothes on fire. She had unwittingly left a box of matches on the chest of drawers, and he must have been playing with them. After she stripped off the nightdress and burning sheet, she and Mrs Williams applied some oil to his hip and stomach, the affected areas. A doctor was summoned and dressed the wounds. He seemed none the worse for his ordeal at first, and was his usual lively self for much of the day, but in the evening he had severe convulsions, and he died from shock next day.

At the inquest on 2 October at the Granada Arms, East Southsea, Mr Williams said that his son had always been fond of playing with matches, and he had often had to stop him from doing so. The coroner told Miss Roe that he trusted this would be 'a caution to her' in future, but exonerated her from blame, saying that she had showed great presence of mind in not running off screaming, as most other girls of her age might have done, but stayed behind to remove the burning garments, severely injuring her hands in the process.

30 SEPTEMBER   **1929**   Leslie Reynolds (30) was found dead in his cell at Portsmouth gaol. He had been arrested in Portsmouth on 28 September on a charge of drunkenness, and death was believed to be due to cerebral haemorrhage.

OCTOBER

Hot off the presses: the inside of a London printers (in this case, the *Daily Telegraph*) in the last years of Victoria's reign. Walter Annett (37), a printer of Charlotte Street, Portsmouth, was found floating in the Thames in October 1889, a sodden London newspaper in his pocket.

1 OCTOBER   **1936**   Two RAF aeroplanes collided above the Solent, and one dived into the sea. The sole occupant, Pilot Officer John Rupert Stephenson, stationed at the RAF station at Gosport, was killed, but the other machine landed safely. The accident had been seen by an army officer from the steamer *Sandown*, which was crossing from Portsmouth to Ryde. He told the master, who altered his course to go to the pilot's assistance. A boat was lowered and Stephenson was taken on board, but a doctor crossing to the Isle of Wight found that he was dead. The body was transferred to a RAF tender in mid-Solent and taken on to Calshot.

2 OCTOBER   **1891**   An inquest was held at Portsmouth Town Hall on Charles Reading (60), a Royal Artillery pensioner, who lived with his nephew at Oxford Street, Landport, and had generally enjoyed good health. On the previous day, after playing with the children in the house, he left at about 8 p.m., saying he was going to get some supper. At about 9.25 p.m. he was seen by Charles Pyle, a corn merchant, to fall headlong into the gutter at Commercial Road. As he was just outside a public house, several other people who saw him thought he was drunk. Ryle quickly found a police constable, who took charge of the ailing man; they accompanied him to hospital, but he was dead on arrival. The house surgeon said he had died of heart disease.

3 OCTOBER   **1898**   Emma Bonney (48) was charged at Portsmouth Police Court with throwing herself into the sea with attempt to kill and murder herself the previous day. John Morris, a labourer, said he was at the Sally Port after midnight when he heard somebody call out, 'Save me!' He looked down the steps into the water and saw her standing on the steps, saying she had tried to drown herself. He asked her where she lived, and she gave an address in Stone Street, saying she did not want to return there as she had been badly beaten. He took her to the police station instead. Dr Maybury, who examined her, said she was drunk and 'very excitable'. On the application of the police, she was remanded in Kingston Gaol for a week.

4 OCTOBER   **1842**   Alfred Cain, a travelling tinker, was involved in a drunken fraccas and suffered several injuries, including a broken thumb. He died of lockjaw the following week.

5 OCTOBER   **1808**   Lieutenant Butler, quartered at Parkhurst Barracks, drowned himself in the river near Dodner's Hard in what was called 'a sudden fit of derangement'.

6 OCTOBER   **1865**   Eliza Chevis (2) was accidentally poisoned. Her father, a coachman, went to a chemist at Alton for twopence-worth of sweet oil of almonds and syrup of violets, which he used to give his children for colds. He did not see the proprietor, Mr Knight, who was away at the time, and he was served by his apprentice, a boy of about 15. A teaspoonful of the mixture was given to Eliza, who became ill and died within an hour. An assistant in the business said at the inquest at the Duke's Head that the mixture contained essential oil of almonds, less than a teaspoonful of which would cause death.

1871 During the morning two doctors were called to the room of Solomon Norman (56), a cabinet-maker and upholsterer of Above Bar, Southampton. He was unconscious and breathing intermittently, the pupils of his eyes very strongly contracted, and it proved impossible to rouse him. They thought it was a case of narcotic poisoning, and applied a stomach pump, but found the stomach was completely empty. Norman died shortly after 1 p.m. It was known that he had suffered poor health of late, and had been in the habit of taking morphia or laudanum. At an inquest at the George Inn, Southampton, on 10 October, the jury returned a verdict that he died from an accidental overdose of morphia.

7 OCTOBER

1889 Walter Annett (37), a printer of Charlotte Street, Portsmouth, went missing. He left his office at 9.30 a.m., and never returned home. Seventeen days later Thomas Ladbroke, a waterman in London, reported seeing a body floating down the river near Blackfriars Bridge in the morning. It was very decomposed, and he hauled it out and handed it over to the police. In the coat pocket was a newspaper dated 10 October, a receipt for lodging money showing that the deceased had stayed at Pierce's Temperance Hotel, Stamford Street, Blackfriars, on 8 and 9 October, and only a farthing in cash. Edward Annett, who had worked in the same business as his brother, identified the body. At an inquest on 28 October, he said that his brother did not appear depressed when he left home, and did not know of any reason he had for visiting London. An open verdict of 'found drowned' was returned.

8 OCTOBER

1913 William Latham was spending a few days' holiday in Hampshire, and late at night he and a female companion were cycling from Hawley to Farnborough. While turning from Hawley Lane on to the main road, they made a detour to avoid one car but instead crashed straight into another. He was killed outright, but the lady only suffered minor injuries though she was thrown off her bicycle. One of the motorists drove her to her home near Henley-on-Thames.

9 OCTOBER

1861 Elizabeth Caroline Snellgrove (23) had been a cook for seven months to a gentleman's family at a house in Portsmouth Road, Woolston, near Southampton. She occasionally complained of feeling bilious, but had not been seriously ill. Whilst working during the afternoon, she announced that she was suffering from violent pains in her head; the pains became increasingly painful throughout the rest of the day. Next morning she was found dead in bed. Death was ascribed to 'asthenic apoplexy from natural causes', and the inquest jury at Winchester recorded a verdict 'by the visitation of God'.

10 OCTOBER

Portsmouth Road, Woolston, where Elizabeth Snellgrove, a cook, died suddenly in October 1861.

11 OCTOBER

1836 The *Clarendon*, which had left St Kitts in the West Indies on 27 August, arrived at Blackgang beach at around 6 a.m. She had been carrying eleven passengers, seventeen crew, and a cargo of sugar, molasses and rum. A howling gale with very rough seas was blowing, and the vessel broke up in less than ten minutes. Only three of the crew survived, and they owed their lives to the prompt action of a local fisherman, John Wheeler. With a few men on the beach end of a rope and the other tied round his waist, he ran into the surf and called to those left on board to jump. Those who did were dragged to safety on shore. The others were all either drowned or killed by timbers in the surf. Among them were a family of six, Lieutenant Shore, his wife and four daughters, aged between nine months and eighteen. Most of the casualties were buried at Chale churchyard. A lighthouse was built at St Catherine's Point nearby, and completed and first used in March 1840.

12 OCTOBER

1920 Jean Tucker, a young domestic servant from Colchester, appeared before Southampton magistrates, charged with being a stowaway. Dressed as a fireman, she had boarded the steamer *Philadelphia* at Southampton, planning to land at New York and marry Mr Manning, one of the vessel's firemen. Other stowaways had been found and ejected before the ship sailed for America, but she was not discovered until the steamer arrived at New York. A search was made after complaints from third-class passengers that their clothing had been stolen. Two officers saw Manning and another fireman dragging her from the potato locker where she had been hiding throughout the voyage, having been fed by members of the crew. She was fined £30, approximately the cost of the return passage, with the alternative of a month's imprisonment. Manning had already been gaoled in America for contravening aliens' regulations.

13 OCTOBER

1842 An inquest was held on the body of a woman found floating in Stokes Bay. The dead woman was identified as Jane Harding, spinster, a servant at Portsea. There were no marks of violence, and it was assumed that she had taken her own life in 'a fit of despondency' after the end of an unhappy love affair.

14 OCTOBER

1645 Basing House was sacked. Built in the sixteenth century as a palace for Sir William Paulet, 1st Marquis of Winchester, it had 3,800 rooms, was five storeys high, and was said by some to be the greatest private house in England. At the outbreak of the Civil War, it belonged to the 5th Marquis, a supporter of King Charles I. Parliamentary troops attacked the house three times, but on the first two occasions the forces were driven off. A final siege began in August 1645 when 800 troops, led by Colonel John Dalbier, took up position around the walls. During the siege Dalbier used an early form of poison gas, burning wet straw with sulphur and arsenic upwind of the house. Further reinforcements joined the parliamentary forces but the garrison held out until Cromwell arrived with heavy artillery; a summons to surrender was issued on 11 October and rejected, and the Parliamentarian artillery opened fire next day.

The siege of Basing House, after Wenceslaus Hollar, c. 1645.

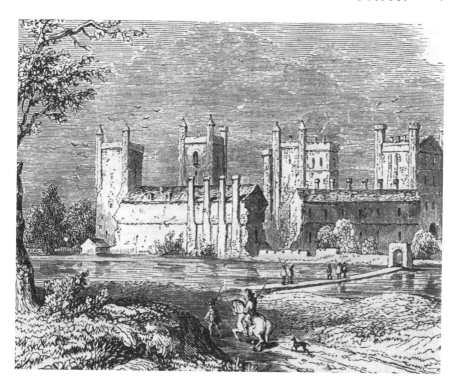

Basing House, sacked by Cromwell's forces in October 1645.

After two days' bombardment the walls were breached, and Cromwell ordered a general assault for daybreak on 14 October. There were too few defenders to have any hope of withstanding the New Model Army, and they were driven back from the outer defences to make a last stand at the Old House gatehouse. At least a hundred, perhaps as many as double that figure, were killed, including soldiers, civilians and priests, and the rest were taken prisoner. Cromwell allowed the troops to plunder valuable goods, including jewels, hangings and furniture worth £200,000. The house was then set on fire, burning for nearly 24 hours until only bare walls and chimneys were left. The ruins were demolished by order of Parliament, with the villagers allowed to remove stones and bricks for their own use. The Marquis of Winchester's estates were confiscated and he was sent to the Tower of London on a charge of high treason, though he was later released, and the site of Basing House was returned to him by King Charles II after the Restoration.

1861 The seven-year-old son of Mr Ursall, an employee at Solent Iron Works, who lived at Cowes, was scalded severely after he accidentally knocked over a full coffee pot on 14 October. He died the next day, in great pain, from the shock to his nervous system.

15 OCTOBER

1855 Abraham Baker (29) was brought before Southampton magistrates, charged with the wilful murder of Naomi Kingswell. They had worked as footman and housemaid respectively for the Revd Poynder and his family at Moira Place, Southampton. On 14 October he shot her dead in the kitchen. It was thought that he had become desperately fond of her, but his feelings were

16 OCTOBER

not reciprocated, and she had told him she wanted to have nothing more to do with him. A new gold wedding ring was found in his purse, indicating that he might have proposed marriage to her but had been spurned, and a letter which he had written to his parents on the morning of the murder, which began, 'This may be the last time I shall have to write to you,' was found in the post office. He was found guilty at Winchester Assizes. While awaiting execution, he made a full confession, in which he claimed he had been 'driven wild with jealousy' by her 'womanish and teasing coquetry'. He was hanged on 8 January 1856.

17 OCTOBER   1933 Flying Officer John Francis Peacock and Leading Aircraftman Harry Foley were both killed when a flying boat crashed in Southampton Water. There were two survivors, Aircraftman O'Connell and Wing Commander Studd, both of whom gave evidence at the inquest at Fawley a month later. O'Connell said that when the pilot tried to take off the machine bounced three times, and he was thrown from the cockpit into the water. Captain Frank Wilkins, an investigating officer of the Accidents Branch of the Air Ministry, had examined the wreckage, and said all the controls were in a serviceable condition. However, he thought the flying boat would be extremely 'nose heavy', making it difficult – if not impossible – for the machine to take off the water. Studd said that he thought the flight had been proceeding smoothly until the plane left the water after 'a longish run', rose a couple of feet and fell back on the water. After a further short run it went up in the air, dropped back and immediately bounced into the air again. He instinctively put his hands down to close the throttle. All he remembered after that 'was a terrible crash and finding myself in the water'. The jury retried a verdict of death by accident due to an error of judgment.

18 OCTOBER   1938 Albert Edward Massey (22) appeared at Winchester Quarter Sessions. He pleaded guilty to charges of stealing a motor boat, a car, an overcoat, and other articles valued together at £215 19s 5d, and breaking into a garage at Fareham. He applied for a dock brief, but when told he had to put up £1, explained that he did not have the money. For the prosecution, Mr Scott Henderson said there were twenty-nine other charges which Massey wanted taken into consideration. He had stolen a motorcycle, using it to tour various seaside towns and committing thefts en route. Having abandoned the machine, he stole another at Gosport, and on it had an accident at Alton. He was taken to the infirmary but escaped, took a fast motor boat at Hamble and was next seen at Shalfleet Creek. The police obtained a motor launch, found him at Newtown Creek and chased him again. Massey's craft was the faster and he got away to Beaulieu River, where he beached the boat and escaped into the forest. He stole a car at Ringwood, and was seen at Fareham two days later by a police constable, who had to jump for his life. At Marlborough, four constables had to jump for it when they tried to stop him. On 13 September, he was arrested at Gloucester.

Massey, who had been married in 1937, had several previous convictions. He was sent to Borstal for three years.

19 OCTOBER   1898 Mrs Ellen Knight was charged at Winchester Quarter Sessions with inflicting grievous bodily harm on Alfred Cooper by striking him with an

Beaulieu, where Albert Massey temporarily evaded police while on the run in October 1938.

earthenware jug at Brading on 1 October. Cooper told the court he was standing outside the Bugle Inn when he received a violent blow on the head and was knocked senseless. He knew the prisoner, and earlier that evening had invited her to have a glass of beer with him. She said that she had acted in self-defence, presumably to fend off any over-familiar attentions from him, but she was found guilty of common assault and sentenced to fourteen days' hard labour.

1884 A case of severe family discord was settled in Portsmouth Police Court **20 OCTOBER**
when Edward Thomas Dodd, a Landport blacksmith, was summoned by his sister-in-law Kate on a charge of having assaulted her on 12 October. In court she claimed that he had scratched her in the face, and tried to strike her. Her husband, Edward's brother Henry, said that Edward had threatened to murder both of them. In his defence, Edward complained that Kate had used 'gross language' towards him, and the father of Edward and Henry said that fighting between them had been going on between them the whole of Saturday afternoon, resulting in Kate threatening to knock his brains out with a poker. The magistrates, perhaps taking the view that they all deserved each other, dismissed the case.

1941 It was reported in *The Times* that 2nd Lieutenant R.E.G. Cox (24), of the **21 OCTOBER**
Indian army, who had arrived in England on sick leave and lived at Fareham, had, as one of twelve men on a capsizing raft as small as a hearthrug, been blistered by sun, and gone without food or drink; he had been stalked by man-eating sharks for five days. One by one the men perished, until only three survived. Cox's normal weight was 13st, but when rescued he weighed only 6st 3lb. He was so blistered and weak that the doctors initially gave up any hope of saving him.

On his way to take up duties in India in January, the merchant ship in which he was travelling was sunk by a German raider in the Atlantic 1,200 miles from land. A raider stopped them and began shelling. Many passengers, including women, were killed. The raider gave them five minutes to take to their boats, most of which were riddled with shell holes and therefore useless. Their craft overturned several times. Each time they got back on board – though nine of them died in the process. One man strapped to the side in a life jacket was washed away, and another who swam after him was killed by a large fish. At last they sighted a Spanish ship and were lifted on board in slings. Later on, the ship picked up a load of about forty-six other survivors and took them to Tenerife. Other survivors, he thought, had reached Montevideo after twenty-three days in an open boat. At Tenerife they were entrusted to a Spanish physician who saved them (including one man who was suffering from gangrene after his leg had been almost bitten off by a shark).

22 OCTOBER   **1874**   An inquest was held at the Lucknow Tavern, Somers Road, Fratton, on Elizabeth Young, aged 4½ months. The daughter of Joseph Young, a Fratton seaman, who lived at Lucknow Street, she had previously been in perfect health. Her mother put her to bed as usual at 7 p.m. on 21 October; when she checked her at 9.30, she found her very pale and cold. She gave her a warm bath but to no avail: the baby died later that night. The doctor and inquest jury returned a verdict of accidental suffocation.

23 OCTOBER   **1818**   Thomas Huntingford (71), who lived with his wife Sarah (61) at Orange Street, Portsea, was killed in his bed during the night. Early the following morning Sarah was found pacing around nervously in the yard outside, dressed only in her nightclothes, saying that she had been attacked and robbed. Thomas was found lying in bed, savagely battered around the head. Sarah told her landlady and neighbours that two men dressed as chimney sweeps had killed him, and she did not raise the alarm as they had threatened to do the same to her. Spots of blood were found on her clothing, and a bloodstained billhook was found in the coalhole which was evidently the murder weapon. She was tried at Winchester Assizes on 5 March 1819 and hanged at Gallows Hill three days later.

24 OCTOBER   **1957**   Douglas Owen d'Elboux Miller (65), the headmaster of Boundary Oak School, Widley, a private boarding school near Portsmouth, was found shot dead. At an inquest, two days later, it was reported that he was about to retire but deeply worried about the appointment of his successor. A suicide verdict was returned.

25 OCTOBER

The discovery of the body of Joe Martin, who shot himself at his house in Kingsclere in October 1897. (*Illustrated Police News*)

A HUSBAND'S SUICIDE AT KINGSCLERE

1897   Mrs Martin (23) walked out on her husband Joe (64), to whom she had been married for four years. It had been a stormy union, and the last straw was a furious argument at their home at Swan Street, Kingsclere, after which she returned to her mother at Deptford. Joe, who had formerly been well known in the racing world, was seen by a neighbour soon afterwards that day 'in an excited state'. A shot from the house was later heard, and when police made a forced entry into the premises on 28 October they found that Joe was dead. At the inquest the following day, a verdict of suicide was returned.

1948 The body of Captain Robert Paterson (35) of the Royal Marines was found on board HMS *King George V* with a single shotgun wound. An inquest was held at Portsmouth on the following day. The coroner, Mr P.H. Childs, said he was in no trouble of any kind, but suffered from some form of delusion of inferiority which might have caused him to take his own life.

26 OCTOBER

1798 The novelist Jane Austen wrote rather cruelly to her sister Cassandra about the Revd Henry Hall of Monk Sherborne, whose wife 'was brought to bed yesterday of a dead child, some weeks before she expected, oweing [sic] to a fright. – I suppose she happened unawares to look at her husband.'

27 OCTOBER

Jane Austen, author of a rather uncharitable comment about a local clergyman in Monk Sherborne.

1820 Some scaffolding in Southampton High Street collapsed. One workman had his thigh broken in two places, and another sustained severe internal injuries. It was only a few months since the same men had received severe contusions through a fall of part of the front of the same house, and they had only just recovered.

28 OCTOBER

Southampton High Street, scene of a scaffolding accident in October 1820.

1887 The lugger *Pride of the Sea*, which had sailed from Deal, Kent, and was cruising in the Channel, sought shelter along the coast of the Isle of Wight during a strong north-westerly gale, and was thrown onto the rocks at Yellow Ledge, Shanklin. She was completely wrecked and five men died, namely Captain

29 OCTOBER

John Moss, William and Charles Moss, all members of the same family, plus Charles Selth and Henry Aldie. Their bodies were washed up along the beach between Shanklin and Sandown.

30 OCTOBER   1900   Margaret Welch (43) was charged at Portsmouth Police Court with being drunk and disorderly in Queen Street, Portsea, on 27 October, and with exposing her one-month-old daughter in such a manner as to cause her unnecessary suffering. Constable Downing said he saw her dropping the baby on the ground, and he took them to the police station. The child was inadequately clad, and its limbs were blue with cold; it was suffering from exposure, and ravenously hungry. The woman had just served a fourteen-day sentence for sleeping in an outhouse. She was given a further twenty-one days' hard labour.

31 OCTOBER   1893   Minnie Bowdill (19), a servant at North End, Portsmouth, was charged at Portsmouth Police Court with attempting to commit suicide. She was employed at the time by Mrs Bayer, who told the court that Miss Bowdill entered her service in January, and on 4 October was given notice to leave. On 26 October Mrs Bayer was in the kitchen when the servant came downstairs and said to her, 'Oh, what shall I do? I have poisoned myself'. Mrs Bray found that she had swallowed some carbolic acid, and made her drink several cups of warm mustard and water, and remained with her until it took effect, then sent for medical assistance. Mr Weston, who examined her, confirmed that her mouth had been burned by corrosive acid. When asked why she had done such a wicked thing. Miss Bowdill said she was tired of life, and did not want to leave her place of employment. Mrs Bray said she had become 'somewhat unsteady', and taken to returning home late. The prisoner's sister said that she had had an unhappy childhood, but a married sister of theirs had agreed to receive and take care of her, whereupon she was discharged from custody.

NOVEMBER

The medical officers' mess at the Royal Naval Hospital, Haslar. (© *Nicola Sly*)

1 NOVEMBER **1847** An inquest was held at the Swan Inn, Petersfield, on the body of Fanny Harrison (7) of Rake. On the evening of 29 October she and her elder sister Louisa were coming back from school to their home at Rake. They had been picking up beech nuts. Suddenly, Fanny called to Louisa in a panic, saying she had swallowed one: a horse or a cow had come along and frightened her, and a nut went down her throat as she was jumping over the stile. Louisa ran to the nearest house to get her some water in an attempt to dislodge it, got her to a friend's house and called medical help, but it was too late. The surgeon, George Peskett, told the inquest that, when he examined her throat, her breathing was laboured and he could tell from the symptoms that some foreign matter was responsible, but he could not detect its exact position. She died before he could operate, and at the post-mortem he found the nut lodged in her windpipe.

2 NOVEMBER **1859** Mary Elsley, wife of the landlord of the Royal Military Hotel, Aldershot, died suddenly. Her husband was also responsible for managing the canteen in the camp and was normally absent from the hotel during the daytime, leaving his wife in charge. At about midday she asked a servant, the only one on duty in the house at the time, to take charge of the bar for a short time while she went upstairs. About ten minutes later her brother-in-law suddenly arrived at the hotel. Mr Browning, a lodger at the hotel who helped out occasionally at the bar, called out to the servant to call a doctor, as Mary was unwell. Dr Rentzeh arrived almost at once, but within a few minutes Mrs Elsley was dead – in Browning's bedroom. At the inquest on 5 November at Aldershot, he said that she had come into his room complaining of pain in her head and then collapsed. He caught her in his arms and placed her in the bed, with some difficulty.

In reporting the inquest, the *Hampshire Telegraph* stated that 'the evidence cannot be given in detail', but said that the servant's evidence differed materially from Browning's account, and that of Dr Rentzeh showed that much of it was 'entirely false'. The jury passed a verdict to the effect that Mrs Elsley died from effusion of blood on the brain, caused by sudden shock or fright', while expressing total disbelief in the truth of Browning's statement.

3 NOVEMBER **1934** Constable Ernest Cummins (41), who had served with the Hampshire Constabulary for twenty years and was stationed at Portsmouth, was killed when his bicycle came into collision with a light motor van.

4 NOVEMBER **1899** William Baker (24), labourer, was charged at Winchester Assizes with wounding Henry Robinson at West Tisted on 4 November, with intent to do him grievous bodily harm. It was alleged by the prosecution that he had stabbed Robinson in the left shoulder with a knife in the course of a fight at the New Inn. He was found guilty of unlawful wounding, and sentenced to six months' hard labour.

5 NOVEMBER **1881** Charles Henry Saunders, a gunner in the Royal Marine Artillery, assaulted his wife Caroline in her house at Portsmouth. When he was charged with the offence at the Portsmouth Local District Police Court on 9 November, she said that he came round to her house, struck her over the eye with a key, pulled her about the room by her hair, kicked and bit her. Evidence as to her injuries was corroborated by two witnesses. Mr Saunders was sentenced to four months' imprisonment with hard labour.

1881 The same session of the Portsmouth Police Court heard the case of Jane Searle. She had been summoned for having used threatening language towards Samuel Armstrong, who was the verger of St Mark's Church, North End. During the last two months Searle had caused considerable disturbance at the church, and she had to be ejected several times. This was repeated on this day: while standing outside the building, the defendant told the complainant that he 'had put her out to please the vicar'. Armstrong said he had found the summons, which had been posted up at the vicar's door. In cross-examination Mr Blake, who was appearing for the defendant, told the court that there had been a dispute about a cushion which the defendant had placed in the church. She had subsequently received a letter from the Bishop to say that after she had once placed a cushion in a church she could not legally remove it. In her fury, she ran up to the church and tried to destroy the cushion. 6 NOVEMBER

The vicar, the Revd S. Ledbitter, said that the defendant had induced him to believe that she was mad. He knew that she had placed a cushion in one of the free seats, and she had annoyed him in the most unwarrantable way, so he had sent her money amounting to its estimated value three or four times, but every time it had been returned to him. In the process she had annoyed the congregation so much that he thought it would be necessary to take steps to put a stop to her conduct, otherwise he feared she might be taken away and confined in an asylum. The defendant said the cushion was worth 30s, and she wanted to take it back. She promised to refrain from causing any more disturbance, and the magistrates directed her to enter into her own recognisance of £20 to keep the peace for three months.

1815 Mr Cole, of the South Hants Yeoman Cavalry, was returning on horseback from the assembling and exercise of his troop when he fell off his horse at Buckland, near Lymington and ruptured a blood vessel in the head. He died the following night. 7 NOVEMBER

1807 Adjutant John Faden, of the Royal Marines, spent some time in the sole company of Elizabeth Stapleford (18) at the Marine Barracks, Portsmouth, a meeting which ended in his being charged with assault and rape. Miss Stapleford was one of three daughters of a widow, and they helped to support their mother by taking in needlework. She and Faden had become quite attached to each other, and they often went for walks with each other, unchaperoned. On the evening in question, one thing apparently led to another, and he appeared at Winchester Assizes on 11 March 1808 charged with rape. He pleaded not guilty, and she said she had resisted his attentions 'to the utmost'. For the defence, Mr Burroughs read a letter in court which she had admitted was in her handwriting. Addressed to Faden at the barracks, it was dated 3 November 1807, unsigned, but took the form of a sonnet, including among its fourteen lines: 8 NOVEMBER

Naval Barracks,
Portsmouth,
c. 1910. Royal
Marine John Faden
was accused by
Elizabeth Stapleford
of assault and rape.

Return, return, my Faden, Oh! Return;
'Tis thy love calls thee, 'tis thy love that mourns,
Oh! Come and cheer me, with one kind embrace,
Lest pity smile upon thy heav'nly face,
Contented then, I'd join my heart to death,
And gaze, and love thee, 'till I lose my breath.

Her case was further weakened by the fact that several witnesses, who had been in adjoining apartments that evening, said they heard no noise at the time of the 'pretended assault'. In summing up, Serjeant Marshall said that the letter was 'nearly an answer', and at least showed that she was ready to fall into his arms. The jury had to decide whether she had been 'ravished by brutal force', or whether she met the prisoner's embrace halfway. The jury, believing the latter, immediately returned a verdict of not guilty.

9 NOVEMBER **1859** At Hampshire County Petty Sessions, Peter Norman, a labourer, was sentenced to two months' hard labour at Winchester gaol for stealing 4lb of bread, a knife and a basket at Tadley; another labourer, Jesse Neville, was fined £1, including costs, for stealing one gallon of bean meal at Stratfield Saye.

10 NOVEMBER **1800** Mr James Grainger, a naval cadet at Portsmouth, died after fighting a duel with Mr Thomas Stapleton, of the 20th Foot Regiment. In October they had quarrelled, with Grainger calling Stapleton a coward and making derogatory comments about Ireland, the latter being Irish. He then brought a pair of swords so they could settle the dispute by fighting. Stapleton was suffering from rheumatism and did not want to fight; the captain saw what was happening and took the swords away, and they made it up. They remained friends until

5 November, when a further quarrel ensued and Grainger insisted they fight a duel with pistols next day at the Blue Posts Inn. Grainger fired first and missed, but Stapleton had better luck, and his adversary fell to the ground. 'I hope you are not hurt, my dear fellow,' he told the recumbent loser, 'recollect you have brought it on yourself.'

Unfortunately, Grainger died from his injuries four days later. When Stapleton appeared at Winchester Assizes on 2 March 1801, the judge told the jury that if two people quarrelled in the height of anger, fought, and either of them fell as a result, it was a case of manslaughter. If they met in consequence of a challenge, and one was killed, it was wilful murder. The jury returned a verdict of manslaughter, the prisoner was sentenced to six months' imprisonment, and was fined 1s.

11 NOVEMBER

1890   George Stanley (46), a Gosport labourer, set fire to a stack of straw and a stack of hay, the property of John Henry Drewitt, of Fareham. He pleaded guilty at Winchester Assizes on 11 December. Several times he had asked people for work, the prosecution said, and as he could not get any he vowed that he was not going to walk the roads any longer. Mr Justice Grantham said it was the act of 'a base character towards a man who had done him no harm', and gave him eighteen months' hard labour.

12 NOVEMBER

1875   An inquest was held on the body of Minnie Rosina Fleming, aged four months. She had been found dead in bed beside her mother at their home in Noble Court on 10 November. The mother awoke at 3 a.m. to find the baby sleeping normally, but on waking again four hours later saw she was dead. The surgeon, Mr Morley, said he was sure it had been a case of accidental suffocation.

13 NOVEMBER

1723   The 'Waltham Blacks', a gang of bandits, were tried at the Court of the King's Bench, London. They were the most notorious villains to fall foul of the 'Black Act', which had been passed earlier that year, making it a capital offence to appear armed in a park or warren, or to hunt or steal deer with faces blackened or otherwise disguised. It did not stop a group of seven men from blacking their faces and visiting the parks of the gentry in Hampshire, where they stole deer and shot dead the Bishop of Winchester's keeper on Waltham Chase. Among the gang were Richard Parvin, an innkeeper, two brothers, Edward and John Pink, who had followed the trade of carters, and James Ansell, a highwayman, all of whom came from Portsmouth. The others, Robert Kingshell, James Anstel, and Henry Marshall, who killed the keeper, came from Surrey. After being captured they were taken into custody and lodged at Newgate. All were found guilty and hanged at Tyburn on 4 December.

'A very short, though important lesson, may be learnt from the fate of these unhappy men,' remarked *The Newgate Calendar*. 'Idleness must have been the great source of their lawless depredations, which at length ended in murder. No man, however successful in the profession, can expect to get as much profit by deer stealing, as by following his lawful business. The truth is, that, in almost every instance, it costs a man more pains to be a rogue than to be honest. Exclusive of the duties of religion, young persons cannot learn a more important maxim than that in the scripture, "the hand of the diligent maketh rich."'

14 NOVEMBER 1896 Dick Linnington (72), a retired labourer, was found dead with his head in a water butt in Percy Shephard's garden at Barton's Village, Newport, where he was lodging. Linnington had been suffering from cancer of the neck, and the relieving officer had been to see about removing him to the workhouse, though he was firmly against such an idea. At an inquest at the White Lion, Coppin's Bridge, Newport, several witnesses said that there was a towel around his neck when he was pulled out, and he might have fallen in. There was nothing to show that he had intended to take his own life, and a verdict of accidental death was returned.

15 NOVEMBER 1910 In the morning, John Alister Damant (20), a former Sub-Lieutenant of the Royal Navy at Cowes, serving in HMS *King Edward VII*, was found dead in bed at the Royal Pier Hotel, Southsea. A bottle of chloroform was found beside his body, which was identified by his brother. He had been staying at the hotel for the last five days and was apparently in good health, although there was some suggestion of minor heart trouble. Six weeks previously, while staying in Edinburgh, he had made an attempt to take his own life, but then promised his family he would not do so again. After that he had been sent to Haslar Hospital, and invalided from the service. There was a family history of insanity and two of his uncles had lost their reason.

Damant had no financial problems, and after leaving the service he was reasonably well off. He had purchased the chloroform from a local chemist the day before his death, saying he wanted it for experimental purposes. A post-mortem by Dr Taylor of Southsea revealed that he had died from suffocation, and had a diseased heart, which might have affected his mental condition. A verdict of suicide while of unsound mind was returned.

16 NOVEMBER 1874 Private Thomas Smith (20) of the 20th Hussars was executed at Winchester Gaol. On 12 September he had shot and killed Captain John Bird at Aldershot Barracks. The previous day, he had been reprimanded for leaving ranks without permission, and when he repeated the offence he was confined to barracks for seven days for 'insubordinate conduct on parade'. As he was escorted to the guardroom, he muttered, 'he won't give me any more bloody seven days'. Although the defence argued at his trial on 28 October that there had been no malice aforethought and that it was an accident, the prosecution and jury declared otherwise.

17 NOVEMBER 1871 An inquest was held at Titchfield on Freddy (10), Willie (9), and Augusta Hinton (7 or 8). The boys were the stepchildren of Mrs Alice Hinton (37), while the girl was her daughter, born before her marriage to John Hinton, a former soldier and now a saddler. The woman, a habitual drunkard, regularly neglected them, sometimes leaving them for the whole

day with nothing to eat but bran. She had been summoned to the Fareham magistrates' court on 16 November on a charge of cruelty, and that morning their father went to buy the boys some boots. While he was out the neighbours heard screaming, and one of them burst open the back door. As she did so, Willie ran out bleeding from a wound in the cheek, and said his brother and sister had been cut.

The police forced an entry into the house, and found Mrs Hinton bleeding from a wound in the throat, obviously self-inflicted. Freddy was lying dead upstairs, clutching a halfpenny in his fingers, and Augusta, holding some sweets, had also been killed, their heads almost severed. Willie was taken into a neighbour's house, but only survived for another two hours. The mother's wound was not serious, but she struggled so violently that the neighbours had difficulty in dressing it properly. After it was stitched up she was taken to Fareham by the police, appeared before the magistrates, and was then removed to the county lunatic asylum. At the inquest her husband said she had been summoned three weeks earlier for neglecting the children, and she thought he was the cause. Two letters were found in the house, in which she reproached him for having treated her and his previous two wives badly, telling him he had brought her to this, 'and may the Lord forgive you for what you have caused me to do.' At the police station, she said he had told her that the sooner she and the children were 'out of the way', the better.

She was tried at Winchester on 29 March, when evidence convinced the jury that she was guilty but insane and therefore not responsible for her actions. The judge sentenced her to be detained in prison during Her Majesty's pleasure. As she was moved to the cells by a female warder she struggled violently, and her screams could be heard some distance away.

1814 Six horses from Bitterne Farm, Southampton, were brought to the harbour to be dipped in salt water, as they had been bitten by a mad dog. On the previous evening a horse and a cow had both died after showing symptoms of hydrophobia. **18 NOVEMBER**

1897 Elizabeth Matthews (21), a servant, was charged at Winchester Assizes with trying to conceal the birth of her child by disposing of the dead body at Exton on 11 May. She confessed to having given birth to a stillborn child, and admitted to keeping it for a week 'in case anyone came about it', then burying it in the garden. The judge told her she had acted in a perfectly straightforward manner. He added that the police often seemed to think 'that no young woman ought to have a baby illegitimately, unless they were acquainted with the fact in some way or other'. The jury found her not guilty; in discharging her, the judge said he was sorry she had been put in her present position. **19 NOVEMBER**

1930 An inquest was held at Romsey on the body of Thomas Fern (32), one of a group of motor bandits from Christchurch who had recently convicted of housebreaking at Hampshire Quarter Sessions and sentenced to five years' penal servitude. He was killed while jumping from a train on the line **20 NOVEMBER**

Convent Walk,
Christchurch.
Several thieves who
lived in the area
were sentenced for
housebreaking in
November 1930.

between Eastleigh and Romsey, en route to Dartmoor Prison, in an effort to escape. During the journey, the four convicts asked Robert Flitton, the warder from Winchester who was in charge, to be allowed to use the lavatory. Fern went first, with Flitton standing behind him – it was then noticed that Fern had managed to get both hands free from his handcuffs. Flitton got hold of Fern and they struggled, but Fern escaped and rushed down the corridor, opened the carriage door, and jumped out. According to Dr Ralph Clarke Bartlett, the prisoner must have injured himself when the end of one of the sleepers struck him in the chest, and death would have been instantaneous. The coroner said he thought that Fern was trying to make a getaway, and he did not believe it was suicide. A verdict of accidental death due to misadventure was returned.

21 NOVEMBER   **1898**   Frederick Dowling (63), a tailor, and his wife Charlotte (67) appeared at Winchester Assizes, charged with the manslaughter of their son, also called Frederick (34), at Winchester, between 1 May and 24 July. The son was blind and 'of weak intellect', and, according to the prosecution, the parents had been neglecting him 'in such a manner that he simply rotted away from wounds which they had left uncared for, and died'. All three lived, slept, worked and ate in a room 12ft by 10ft, which they rented at 1s 9d per week, and in which the son lay until he was taken to the Winchester workhouse four days before his death. In June Mr Dowling the elder sent for a doctor – to treat himself, not his son, for rheumatism. The doctor then saw the son, who was lying on a piece of sacking on a bed which was so rotten that the pieces had to be swept up and thrown away. He was covered with bedsores and vermin, with wounds so deep that the spinal cord and some of the ribs were visible. He was plainly dying, and was only sent away at that point. The nurse who looked after him promptly contracted typhoid fever, which in her view was no coincidence. A neighbour testified to

hearing the unfortunate man moan and shout, 'Mother, you wicked woman!' He was fully conscious and 'sensible' up to the day of his death, attributed to shock to the nerves caused by the constant discharges, pain and irritation, and by poisonous gases exhaling from the sores.

Mr and Mrs Dowling denied all charges of neglect, claiming that their son was very stubborn, and asserting that it was the carbolic bath he was given at the workhouse which killed him. Mrs Dowling said she had given him medicine and had not sent for a doctor because she did not want him taken away to the infirmary. They were found guilty of gross and cruel neglect, and Mr Justice Kennedy told them that their son must have suffered fearful agonies, night and day. He took into account their poor position and age, but nevertheless he was sentencing them both to fifteen months' imprisonment with hard labour. 'I shall not serve fifteen days,' Frederick answered. 'It will kill me and it will kill her.'

1859 A railway accident occurred at about midday at Fleetpond Station, near Basingstoke, on the 11 a.m. from Waterloo to Basingstoke, due in at 12.15 p.m. There was dense fog that day, and the officials had a goods train in the station, so they decided to shunt it so the express train could pass safely. The driver probably did not see the signals, or alternatively the parties at the station were unaware of the express train's approach. It crashed into the back of the goods train, and the locomotive of the express train, the tender and guard's van were all destroyed. Several trucks of the goods train were badly damaged. Several of the passengers were screaming, but although several had sustained bruising and shock, there was no loss of life. It was thought that the driver and stoker of the train were aware of the danger as soon as they saw what was happening, and must have thrown themselves down, thus escaping injury. If they had not done so, they would probably have been killed.   22 NOVEMBER

1959 An inquest jury at Havant decided that Mrs Christine Showers (33), of Seagrove Avenue, Hayling Island murdered her husband Charles (59) and their daughter Juliet (7), and set fire to the house. Her death was due to shock and asphyxia from the flames. They also returned verdicts that she murdered her husband with an axe, and her daughter by knocking her unconscious and setting the building alight. All of the couple's other four children – Susanne (11), Stephanie (9), Amanda (5) and Tony (four months) – survived. The coroner read a statement made by Susanne in hospital, describing the night that 'Mummy went mad'.   23 NOVEMBER

Hayling Island, where Christine Showers killed her husband, daughter and herself in November 1959.

24 NOVEMBER   **1830**   Around this time there were numerous riots by agricultural workers throughout much of Hampshire. Crowds roamed the streets of Andover for several days, and at Barton, five miles away, a mob set light to Sir Henry Wilson's rickyard, burning it to the ground. The fire engine at Andover was sent for, but those in charge refused to let it be taken from the town, as Barton was outside the parish of Andover, and they thought it might soon be needed in the town as well. At Havant, another mob went breaking threshing machines, extorting money and beer from inns on their way. Barton Stacey, near Winchester, the premises of Sir Henry Wilson, were destroyed by the flames, with three large barns, several smaller outbuildings, and ten sacks of wheat set ablaze. About 800 labourers visited villages around Micheldever, breaking every threshing machine they could lay their hands on. Throughout the county, farmers received letters threatening the destruction of their corn and buildings. Near Alresford, a gang of labourers assembled, went to the Grange, assaulted a son of the house when he tried to speak to them about 'the impropriety of their conduct', and became so threatening that a contingent of the military was called from Portsmouth to keep order.

Rioters during the unrest of November 1830, which affected several rural communities throughout the county.

An early nineteenth-century horse-powered threshing machine, one of the inventions of the Industrial Revolution which threatened the jobs of several agricultural workers at the time.

1921 The body of Lieutenant Commander D.F. Jones of the Royal Navy was found on Southsea Common, with a gunshot wound and a revolver beside him. He was taken to hospital but died later that week. An inquest was held at Portsmouth on 2 December. His father, Mr G.F. Jones, a solicitor from Mitcham, said that while in hospital his son expressed sorrow for what he had done. He was on the staff of the Naval Mining School, Portsmouth, but he had been 'fed up' since coming to the area from Scotland: the work was too much for him, and he would have to resign. During the war he had served in the Dover Patrol, in the Atlantic and in the North Sea, took part in the battle of Jutland and in several minor engagements. He had lost a brother during the conflict, and his father was sure that he had never really recovered from the hard work during his time on active service. The coroner, Sir Thomas Bramsdon, expressed his sympathy, and agreed with the view that Jones had taken his life as a result of war strain. A verdict of suicide while of unsound mind was returned.

25 NOVEMBER

1860 Mr Vaughan, an assistant employed by Messrs Padmore and Lane, Ryde, tried to kill himself by cutting his own throat. His landlady heard a strange noise, got up and went into his apartments. She immediately called a doctor. He had not injured himself seriously, and was soon out of danger.

26 NOVEMBER

1875 Tomasso Losi, an Italian butler in the service of the Earl of Northesk, at Longwood House, near Winchester, killed himself. At about 11 a.m. Mr Godwin of Tichborne called on Mr Jacob, a bailiff, and said he had seen a badly wounded man in a nearby field. Jacob fetched his horse and cart, recognised Losi, and took him away. When the Earl was told, he had the dying man taken to hospital. Losi had cut himself with a razor in the throat and stomach, and died about six hours later.

27 NOVEMBER

At the inquest at the County Hospital, Winchester, on 29 November, witnesses said that the deceased had been increasingly dispirited, suffered from ill-health, and complained from pain in his head and side. He asked regularly whether the Earl was likely to go to Italy soon, as he believed he could not survive another winter if he stayed in England. Mary Ann Fields, the Earl's housekeeper, said Losi seemed very childish in his ways, and she treated him like a child, never thwarting him, as he was 'a passionate man'. He would give her little presents, and then take them away so he could give them to others. Sometimes the butler seemed afraid of himself, complained that his country was being bitterly oppressed by the French, and always appeared to be irritated or troubled by something. If he thought the other servants were being unkind to him he would shut himself away, and refuse all food. Lord Rosehill said he had seen him recently, and noticed 'a morbid tendency to melancholy and general depression' – to the point where he wondered whether the man was really sane. The jury returned a verdict of 'suicide while of unsound mind'.

28 NOVEMBER   **1931**   Flying Officers Arthur George Teideman and John Burslem MacKenzie, stationed at Gosport, were killed when their machine crashed at Hill Head on the shore of the Solent. The officers, both of whom were dead when removed from the wreckage, were flying a Moth aeroplane. While passing over Hill Head, the machine suddenly nosedived and fell into a garden, just missing Mr Lock, who was working there.

29 NOVEMBER   **1943**   The body of Rose Robinson (62), landlady of the John Barleycorn, Portsmouth, was found dead on her bedroom floor. She had evidently been burgled for the takings, which she kept in her handbag with her, and then strangled after a fierce struggle with her attacker. Nearly four weeks later, as the trail was going cold, police in London arrested Harold Loughans (47), a career criminal who had spent much of his life in prison, for unlawful possession of a pair of new boots which he was trying to sell. When they arrived at the station he mentioned a number of crimes he had recently committed, including a murder at Hampshire about a fortnight earlier. He made a rather sketchy statement admitting that he had killed Mrs Robinson. Just before one of his court appearances he declared he was innocent, and claimed that the police had put words into his mouth when he made the confession.

At the first trial at Winchester early in March 1944 the jury were unable to agree on a verdict, and at a retrial later that month he was found not guilty. He subsequently served further sentences for housebreaking and robbery with violence. In 1963, when he had cancer and less than a year to live, he made another confession in which he admitted that he was indeed the murderer of Mrs Robinson.

30 NOVEMBER   **1940**   Southampton endured heavy air attacks during the Blitz on this and the following night, with 370 killed or seriously injured. Hundreds of families were made homeless, with the suburbs and business district of the city being targeted. Several streets were impassable, and in one road not a single house escaped some damage. The authorities were reported to be taking emergency measures to minimise dislocation of essential services, and food supplies and temporary accommodation was found for thousands of people.

To all and every of the Constables of the Metropolitan Police Force.

Metropolitan Police District, to wit.} WHEREAS

of

(hereinafter called the *Defendant*) hath this day been charged upon Oath before the undersigned, one of the Magistrates of the Police Courts of the Metropolis sitting at the   Police Court in the County of London and within the Metropolitan Police District. For that h ℓ the said Defendant   on the   day of at in the said County and District *Did with divers other evil disposed persons to the number of ten and more unlawfully, riotously and routously assemble and gather together to disturb the Public Peace and did make a great noise, riot and disturbance, to the great terror of his Majesty's subjects therein being, passing and repassing. against the Peace of his majesty the King, his Crown and Dignity*

THESE ARE THEREFORE TO COMMAND YOU and every of you the Constables of the Metropolitan Police Force, in His Majesty's name, forthwith to apprehend the said defendant   and to bring h *im* before Me at the Police Court aforesaid, or before such other Magistrate of the said Police Courts as may then be there, to answer unto the said charge, and to be further dealt with according to Law.

GIVEN under my Hand and Seal, this   Day of   in the Year of Our Lord One Thousand Nine Hundred and   at the Police Court aforesaid.

SCHED. I.—No. 6.
—
WARRANT
First instance.

2000-5-01. M.P.   (120)

Above: A typical Metropolitan warrant. Harold Loughans was arrested in the capital in November 1943, and quickly confessed to the barbaric murder of Rose Robinson.

Left: A memorial to the civilian dead of Southampton during the Second World War.

The condemned cell at Newgate Prison: the 'Waltham Blacks' were imprisoned in Newgate
and executed in November 1723,

DECEMBER

Doctors battle to save a patient's life at the beginning of the twentieth century. Major Coates Phillips's mother-in-law was rushed to a room like this one after an incident on 31 December 1907.

1 DECEMBER   **1950** Rear-Admiral Worsley Gibson (68), and his wife, Phyllis (61), were found dead at their home, Greenmoor Cottage, East Boldre. He was lying on the kitchen floor, his wife was in a sitting position on a settee in the drawing room, and a double-barrelled gun was found lying in the kitchen. At an inquest on 5 December at Lymington, Dr Hamish Allan said that the Admiral had suffered from a depressive condition some years previously. He had recently been in hospital for an undisclosed condition and apparently responded well to treatment, but a week before being discharged he had had a recurrence of depression. An X-ray on 28 November revealed that he had a duodenal ulcer, about which he had been warned. In his condition, any trifling little domestic incidents would have been enough 'to produce severe agitation'. The jury returned a verdict that he murdered his wife and then committed suicide while the balance of his mind was disturbed.

2 DECEMBER   **1932** William George Simmonds (36), a London shoemaker, was found guilty of shooting at Arthur Weeks, a jeweller, and John Grover, his assistant, at Weeks' shop, Elm Road, Southsea, with intent to cause grievous bodily harm. The bullet aimed at Weeks was stopped by the buckle of his braces, and Grover was shot and wounded when he went to his aid. Simmonds was described as a violent and dangerous criminal whose activities in the past had extended across several countries. His previous convictions included a five-year sentence for robbery in America, and three years for throwing vitriol on a bank messenger. Although he pleaded not guilty, he was sentenced to prison for eight years.

3 DECEMBER   **1936** William Thomas Alexander, a railway worker of Golden Common, near Winchester, was charged with attempting to murder his wife and also with attempting suicide. A jury at the Winchester Assizes found him unfit to plead, and he was ordered to be detained during His Majesty's Pleasure.

4 DECEMBER   **1932** Two young officers attached to No. 7 (Bomber) Squadron, RAF, at Worthy Down, Winchester, were involved in an accident over Southampton Water. Pilot Officer R.J. Berens was killed, and Flying Officer E.D. Bishop was left in a very critical condition. Both were associated with the Hampshire Aeroplane Club, with its headquarters at Hamble, and in the afternoon they took a club machine out for a flight over Southampton. They crashed near Netley and came down heavily into the water. A speedboat belonging to the British Power Boat Company was nearby, and hurried to the rescue. Both men were taken to the pier at Southampton; an ambulance drove them to the Royal Southampton Hospital, but Berens was dead on arrival. It had been a fine day with good visibility, and the assumption was that mechanical failure was probably responsible.

5 DECEMBER   **1864** George Broomfield, a butler at a house near Alresford, aged about 47, died in the South Hampshire Infirmary, Southampton. Two days earlier Frederick Colburne, who lived at Shirley Common, went to buy some beer while his wife Caroline, who was six months' pregnant, was preparing supper. She

had been a lady's maid at the same house, and Broomfield came apparently to pay his respects – but in fact his intention was try to persuade her to run away with him to America. When Mr Colburne returned, he found to his horror that the butler had shot her dead with a pistol and then turned the weapon on himself. When asked why he had done so, he said he did it from love, and that nobody could know what he had suffered during the last nine months. He had apparently considered himself very much in love with her; it was about nine months since she had married Mr Colburne. When he was admitted to the infirmary, he told the house surgeon that some years earlier he had been shot in the head, and since then he had suffered from fits of mental derangement. After lingering in agony, he died less than two days after committing the murder.

(This version of events is taken from the *Daily News*. According to other newspapers, Broomfield made a full recovery, was tried at Winchester Assizes for wilful murder on 17 July 1865, found guilty and was sentenced to be hanged).

1886   George Edmunds, a potter, was charged by Fareham magistrates with having refused to leave the Railway Hotel, Fareham, on 28 November, when requested to do so by Ernest Stammers, the landlord, as well as for being drunk and disorderly in Grove Road, and for assaulting Constable Scott. At about 9 p.m. that evening, Edmunds, and his drinking partner, George Davis, were arguing in the bar and it came to a scuffle. The landlord asked them to desist and Davis left at once, while Edmunds was persuaded to go home quietly. After leaving, he returned to the front bar and stayed there a quarter of an hour, behaving abusively towards Stammers, who had recently dismissed his brother, a former barman, from the hotel. He was again persuaded two or three times to leave, and after his brother whispered something in his ear they went away. By this time Edmunds seemed very drunk and excitable; he was using abusive language to everybody. He had to be forcibly removed from the bar, and after he was taken outside he struck at Constable Scott with his walking cane. When taken into custody he kicked Scott on both legs and in the head, and bit Constable Hawkesworth, who had come to assist. **6 DECEMBER**

The magistrates dismissed the charge for refusing to quit the hotel, but fined Edmunds £1 (or seven days' imprisonment) for drunkenness and disorder, and £2 or twenty-one days for the assault, with fourteen days allowed for payment. It emerged that this was his third conviction for similar behaviour.

1899   John Tighe, an outfitter of Palmerston Road, Southsea, was arrested for using threatening language against his wife Edith. He returned home very drunk and in a quarrelsome frame of mind, smashed a window and told a policeman who arrived on the scene that if he did not take his wife away he would cut her head off. He was charged at Portsmouth Police Court, and bound over in his own recognisance of £50 to keep the peace for six months. **7 DECEMBER**

1876   The troopship *Crocodile* arrived at Portsmouth from Bombay. There had been several deaths on board during the voyage, including that of Veterinary **8 DECEMBER**

Surgeon Paton, of the Army Medical Depot, who killed himself by jumping overboard. Another soldier, who had lost his reason, tried to take his own life the same way but was stopped just in time.

9 DECEMBER   **1899**   Frank Ancell (45), a carter, of Kingston, was charged at Portsmouth Police Court with assaulting his wife Kate two days earlier. He pleaded guilty. She said they had been married about a year, but in the last six months he had only brought home half a crown, and she had to take in mangling to keep him, herself and her children by a former marriage. That day he had returned home drunk, took her by the throat, and brandished a knife, threatening he would 'do for her'. He told the court that he was unable to find work, but helped her with the mangling. The clerk to the magistrates read out a list of previous convictions, and asked her how she came to marry such a man. 'I am sorry from my heart that I did,' she answered, 'and I wish that you could give me a separation. I am afraid of my life for him.' The prisoner was sentenced to one month's hard labour.

10 DECEMBER   **1860**   Charles Paice, a Basingstoke auctioneer, died after an accident. On Saturday 8 December he had been riding on horseback between Benworth and Lasham when the horse fell, threw him off, and kicked him in the thigh. He had to walk some distance to get help. On Sunday he seemed to be making good progress, but he had a relapse the next day. His death caused a vacancy on the town council.

11 DECEMBER   **1960**   The body of Brenda Nash (12), a Girl Guide, who had failed to return to her home at Heston, Middlesex, after a guides' meeting, was found under bushes on marshy land at Yateley Common after a search lasting for several weeks. The gruesome discovery had been made by a boy of twelve, who was playing cowboys and Indians with his two younger brothers. She was still in her uniform, and though no effort had been made to dig a grave, it was apparent that her killer had bent and broken the long grass over the body in a half-hearted attempt at concealment. After a post-mortem, a police officer said that she had died from asphyxiation.

On 12 June 1961 the trial of Arthur Jones (44), a fitter-welder, also from Hounslow, who was accused of her murder, opened at Central Criminal Court. He pleaded not guilty. It was alleged that he had lured her into his Vauxhall on the night of 28 October, driven her to the Camberley district, raped and strangled her, and then hidden the body. Three months later, in March 1961, he was sentenced to fourteen years for raping another Girl Guide in September 1960. After a five-day trial, he was found guilty and sentenced to life imprisonment, to start at the end of the fourteen-year term. Mr Justice Sachs told him that he had 'been found guilty now of two crimes evil to a degree and beyond all adjectives.' An appeal against the sentence was heard in October but dismissed.

12 DECEMBER   **1924**   Douglas Goldsmith (49), an auctioneer, sheep breeder and county councillor, broke into the house of Mrs Chalcraft, his mother-in-law, at Liss

during the night. As his sister-in-law, Miss Chalcraft, was going to bed, he demanded custody of his two children, whom he thought were in the house. Because he was so violent and threatening in his behaviour, the doors were barred against him. While the family telephoned the police, he smashed several windows at the front before driving away in his car.

When the case came to court at Winchester Assizes on 21 February 1925 Miss Chalcraft said they had been expecting him to come to the house, as she was aware that papers had been served on him that day from the Divorce Court giving his wife possession of their two children pending divorce proceedings (which were in progress). Goldsmith denied that he had been near the house that night, saying that the whole case for the prosecution was based upon perjured evidence procured by his mother-in-law out of vindictiveness against him. He declared on oath that he had never left his house during the evening, and called on his secretary to corroborate the evidence. Nonetheless, he was found guilty and sentenced to nine months' imprisonment.

1888 John Higgins (32), a former grocer at Deptford, was in financial difficulties. He had borrowed £60 from a young woman of his acquaintance, but became worried and depressed when he was unable to pay it back. On 8 November he knocked at the door of a coachman at Deane, near Basingstoke. His throat had been cut, and he said it was the result of an attack that had been made on him by a gang of strange men while he was on the road. He was taken to the Union Infirmary, and then to Winchester Hospital. At the Infirmary he confessed to having inflicted the injuries on himself, and he could give no reason for having done so. Although the wounds in his throat healed quickly, the inhalation of the discharge from the wounds brought on an inflammation of the lungs, and he died in the evening. At an inquest on 15 December, a verdict of suicide while in a state of temporary insanity was recorded. 13 DECEMBER

1858 Thomas Banks, a former landlord of the Rose and Chapter Inn, and his wife, Emma, appeared at the Guildhall, Andover, charged with the murder of William Parsons, a draper and outfitter. His body had been found face down in a field alongside the road about half a mile from the town on the night of 22 November; he had been bludgeoned to death with a large ash stick, which was found nearby covered in blood and hair. As his clothes were covered in frost, it was assumed that he had been there all night. His watch and a purse containing £3 12s 6d were found in his pocket, so robbery was evidently not the motive. 14 DECEMBER

Mr and Mrs Banks had both been seen in the area that evening. About a month earlier Mrs Banks had taken a dress from Parsons's shop, but whether she had stolen it or been allowed to take it on approval was never established. Mr Banks and Parsons were said to have had 'warm words' about the dress, and allegations of an affair, or at least familiarity, between Mrs Banks and the draper were made. The couple were arrested at their home on suspicion of murder on the 26 November, as they were holding a birthday party for one of their children. The prisoners appeared at Winchester Assizes on 1 March

1859 before Mr Baron Watson, and over forty witnesses were subpoenaed for the prosecution. However, the evidence was purely circumstantial, and the prisoners were discharged.

15 DECEMBER   **1874**   An inquest was held at the United Britons Inn on the body of George Harvey, aged five months, son of Thomas Harvey, a seaman, of Grove Street. About seven weeks earlier, it was said, the child 'broke out' all over the head and face, but his mother thought he was only teething, and did not think it serious enough to call in the doctor. She gave the infant dill water, magnesia, and Stedman's powders, and applied Holloway's ointment to his face. Three days earlier she saw that the gums were very swollen; still thinking the infant was teething, she sent for a packet of teething powders.

When the coroner told her that she must have known the child badly needed medical attendance, she said that her husband was away, she was very poor, and had no friends in the town. Nevertheless, he insisted, if she had advised the parish authorities of her desperate situation they would have provided her with a doctor. She called on Dr Bencraft on 14 December: he had made a superficial examination of the body, and found it to be very thin. He too said that she should have sought medical advice at an earlier stage, but could not say whether the child would have recovered under medical treatment. The jury returned a verdict of 'death from natural causes', but agreed that medical aid should have been obtained long before.

16 DECEMBER   **1899**   William Rose of Twyford Avenue, Stamshaw, was summoned before the Portsmouth Magistrates' Bench for not keeping a dangerous dog under proper control. Earlier in the week, when unsupervised, it had bitten a boy employed by the Corporation in the thigh. He was fined costs of 13s, and ordered to have the dog destroyed.

17 DECEMBER   **1895**   Reports during the evening that a soldier had been killed on the railway line at Copnor led to the discovery of a mutilated body on the line, which had literally been cut to pieces by a train. The police collected as much of the remains as possible and took them to the mortuary, but some portions were missing, and it was thought they must have become entangled with the locomotive and been carried further along the line. The dead man was identified as Sergeant John Daintith (42), of the Mounted Military Police, stationed at Colewort Barracks, Portsmouth. A family man with a wife and two sons, aged 4 years and 12 months respectively, he had been killed by the 5.30 p.m. train from Portsmouth to Netley.

At the inquest at Portsmouth Town Hall on 19 December, his widow said he had seemed slightly depressed for a couple of days, but she did not know why. In the morning he had complained of feeling ill, and said, 'I think I'll lay down and die'. Nevertheless, there was nothing else to point to suicide. In the afternoon, he left the barracks, saying he was going to the town station to make enquiries about a parcel which he should have received from Aldershot on Saturday. After the jury had returned an open verdict, the coroner pointed out that this was the second such death on the railway within a few months, and said the railway companies needed to make the line more secure in order to minimise the possibility of any further such accidents.

1926 The body of the Revd Robert Brook Harrison, curate of St Mark's Church, Farnborough, was found in his room at the vicarage in the morning. An empty bottle, which had contained poison, a partly-written sermon, and two letters, one to his mother and the other to the Revd Lord Mountmorres, vicar of St Mark's, were found beside him. He was in his early thirties and had been at Farnborough for about a year. An inquest was held on 20 December by Major H.M. Forster, coroner for North Hampshire. Dr G. Hunter Dunn said that the deceased had swallowed enough prussic acid to kill sixteen people. The Revd Lord Mountmorres described him as 'particularly sane, but [he] was subject to occasional violent paroxysms of depression, in which he questioned his own fitness for the vocation'. He had previously had a fit of depression about the end of October, and was persuaded to go away on leave for a time, after which he returned apparently much happier than he had seemed for some years. A verdict of suicide while temporarily insane was recorded.

18 DECEMBER

St Mark's Church, Farnborough. The curate, the Revd Robert Harrison, took his life on 18 December 1926.

Farnborough, St Mark's Church

1894 A fire broke out at the palace in Winchester, designed by Christopher Wren for King Charles II, left unfinished and converted into barracks to accommodate 2,000 infantry. Soon after midnight, flames were discovered in the pay office. An alarm was raised, and the fire brigade arrived within a few minutes. Most of the men were in bed and escaped in their trousers and shirts, so nobody was injured. Despite the large amounts of water directed at the building, the flames were swept by a strong south-west wind, soon passed along

19 DECEMBER

the roofs and corridors, and in two hours about 400 rooms were destroyed, as were nearly all their furniture, arms and books. Damage was estimated at several thousand pounds, and the soldiers lost everything except what they stood upright in. Sparks from the conflagration fell right across the city, but fortunately the County Hall, less than a hundred yards away, escaped damage.

20 DECEMBER **1882** Mary Ann Locke was killed by an express train on the London and South-Western Railway at Rowland's Castle. At the inquest two days later, her husband, William, said that in the evening they left the brickyard where she worked to go to Durrant's. They had to cross the railway line to do so. He got on the line through a wicket gate, and she followed. He had passed over one line of metals when he saw that an engine was coming, but assured her that they would have plenty of time to get over. When he reached the next gate, however, he looked around and realised she was no longer behind him. He had never seen a porter at the spot to direct persons to cross, or alternatively to tell them to wait if it was unsafe to go. Joseph Blackhouse of Landport, the engine driver, said that he was driving at about 45mph. When he approached the crossing he could see a figure running, but could not see what it was. He shut off the steam to slow down, and on stopping he found that Mrs Locke had been killed. It was 'folly', he said, for anybody to try and cross while a train was within sight. He had applied his whistle about half a minute before she was knocked down.

1927 Mrs Dorothy Cullen (36), her daughter Peggy Harman (16), and their friend John Abbott (24), all from Southampton, were drowned when their canoe overturned on the river Hamble near Bursledon. A fourth member of the party escaped by pulling himself up the ladder of a houseboat they were trying to reach. A gale had been blowing and the river was quite rough when they got into the canoe, an inquest was told. The vessel probably overturned when one of the women got to her feet as they were nearing the houseboat they were trying to reach.

1882 A body was found in a second-class carriage on the 11.40 a.m. train from London Bridge to Portsmouth. Thomas Ayris, the guard in charge of the train, was calling out to passengers to get their tickets ready for inspection when he noticed the carriage window was broken; he looked in, and saw a respectably-dressed passenger who was apparently asleep. On closer examination, he noticed that the compartment was saturated with blood. The train stopped at Havant so the body could be removed, at which point a flattened bullet fell out of the clothing, and a six-chambered revolver (with five of the chambers still loaded) was found under the seat. The train then continued on its scheduled journey to Portsmouth.

An inquest was opened next day at the Bear Hotel, Havant, under the county coroner, Edgar Goble. The jury went to view the body, which was lying in an outhouse at the hotel, and gave their view that the deceased was about 40 years old. In his pockets were found 6s 3d, a spirit flask containing a small amount of brandy, a second-class ticket from Victoria to Arundel, a bunch of keys, and the second half of a first-class return ticket from Esher to Waterloo. There was also a betting book containing several entries, with one page bearing the entry, 'Having lost all my money, honour, and hope, I only pray for secret,' followed by illegible initials, and the last page, 'Williamson, artist and sculptor, Esher'.

The inquest was adjourned until 5 January 1883, to give friends of the man a chance to come forward. When proceedings were reopened at the hotel Dr Norman, of Havant, said that there had been blood on the right side of the face, wounds on the right temple, and above the left ear. Death had been caused by a gunshot wound, but no evidence could be established as to whether it was self-inflicted or not. Mr Williamson had been contacted by Esher, and could not account for his name being in the book, as he was unaware of any connection with the deceased. The notebook had been examined again, and as German characters were found on one or two of the pages it was thought he might have been German, but no further identification was possible. The jury recorded an open verdict.

1856 Three Italian sailors, Giuseppe Lagava, Matteo Pectrizi, and Giovanni Barbaalo, convicted at Winchester of piracy and of the murder of two men (and the wounding another two) on board the British bark *Globe* while sailing in the Black Sea in July were hanged at the gaol. Immediately after being sentenced, they declared through interpreters that justice had not been done to them.

A few days later, they admitted their guilt, and acknowledged that their punishment was a just one. Lagava, the ringleader, confessed that he was 'the chief sinner, and upon my head will rest the murder of the two sailors for whom we are condemned, as well as of my two poor companions, whom I dragged into it by the hair of their heads. I am guilty, and I deserve death.' Pectrizi claimed he was not guilty of having conspired beforehand to plunder the ship. 'I do not know how the fight began. I only know I was struck and defended myself. I acknowledge it was by my hand the wounds were given of which the sailor died in hospital at Therapis, but I did not do it for plunder. I know I deserve to die, not for piracy, but for worse things I did on the *Globe*. I am a bad man. I have a bad heart. I deserve to die.' He then went on to describe how two years earlier he had killed three persons at Trieste:, a woman with whom he had lived, and two gendarmes who were sent to arrest him. He also tried to murder a man in Constantinople, but his would-be victim had escaped by jumping into the water and swimming away.

24 DECEMBER **1889** George Searl (75) was alleged to have raped his illegitimate six-year-old daughter Maud Bates at the family home in Malthouse Lane, Kingston, Portsmouth. When he was brought before the Crown Court at Southampton on 19 March 1890, he firmly denied the charge. Mr Simonds, defending, commented on what he called the 'utter improbability' of the prosecution's evidence, suggesting that Mrs Bates and the little girl had fabricated the unpleasant story in order to get rid of the prisoner. Nevertheless, he was found guilty and the judge, calling him 'a disgrace to humanity', gave him eighteen months' hard labour.

25 DECEMBER **1898** Private James Whatmore, of the Royal Marine Light Infantry, was stabbed through the heart at Browndown Camp, in the morning, and died within a few minutes. Private Henry Spurrier (23) was arrested on suspicion of murder, and when asked why he had done it, said, 'I only just meant to prick him to buck him up'. At first he appeared dazed, and did not seem to understand that Whatmore was dead. He was taken to Fareham Police Court to be charged, and on the journey he fell asleep, then woke up and asked why he was in custody. When reminded of what he had done, he said, 'Then I am a murderer'.

At his trial at Winchester Assizes on 13 February 1899, the defence placed great emphasis on his epileptic fits, and it was apparent that he had killed Whatmore while in a dazed state shortly after such a seizure. The two men had reportedly been the best of friends. His mother testified to her husband having died insane in an asylum, while one of her daughters was now in a similar institution without any hope of recovery. Medical evidence was produced to show that Spurrier was probably insane at the time and not conscious of the severity of what he was doing. Mr Justice Mathews stopped the case, directing the jury to find the prisoner guilty but insane. Spurrier was sentenced to be detained during Her Majesty's pleasure.

26 DECEMBER **1918** Charles William Rose, who had seen active service in France, was invalided out of the army in 1915. He found employment as a driller in the

Portsmouth dockyard, and lived with his wife and two young sons, aged 2½ years and two months respectively, and his mother-in-law at the latter's house in Portsea. Just before Christmas he had had a difficult and somewhat argumentative time with both women, who invariably sided with each other, and he was also suffering from a painful ear infection. His mother-in-law was so worried by what she called his 'strangeness of manner', that she tried to have him transferred to a hospital or convalescent home, but a health visitor called and decided that he was not ill enough for that.

Victoria Park, Portsmouth, where Charles Rose was arrested in December 1918 after killing his children.

The three adults evidently called a truce over the festive period, and it seemed that everything was back to normal. On the morning of Boxing Day Rose was playing happily with the elder boy. In the afternoon he went to his wife in the kitchen, told her he was going away, that the babies would not 'worry her any more,' and that she was a free woman. When she and her mother asked him what he meant, he assured them that the children were all right, and slipped out of the house, throwing a bloodstained razor in the gutter, later retrieved by a boy who lived nearby. The two women went upstairs to find the children in bed, dead, with their throats cut. He was arrested two days later in Victoria Park, Portsmouth, and gave a false name, but on being arrested and searched at the police station a notebook containing his real name was found in his pocket. He went on trial at the Winchester Assizes in spring 1919, was found guilty of murder but not held responsible for his actions, and ordered to be detained in a criminal lunatic asylum.

1831 Thomas Randal, a shoemaker who had previously been employed as a labourer in the Portsmouth dockyard, and his wife Elizabeth lived in Carpenter's Court, St James's Street, Portsea. Both were alcoholics, and had been drinking heavily since Christmas Eve. Soon after 1 p.m., Mr Randal went outside, saying

27 DECEMBER

loudly, 'I have done it; I have done what I intended to do, and I am now ready for the gallows.' Several people who overheard him, knowing he could be violent when he had had too much to drink, held back, but one, a Mr Tilly, came along and asked exactly what he had done. When Randal repeated himself, Tilly strode into the house, and found Randal's wife lying at the foot of the stairs, covered in blood. He took her shawl off and found a deep wound in the neck below the left ear. After trying to stop the bleeding, he called two doctors, but within a few minutes she had perished from loss of blood. A bloodstained knife was removed from upstairs.

Mr Randal was taken into custody, and an inquest was held that evening at the Three Crowns, St James's Street, at which a verdict of wilful murder was returned. On the following day he was told he would be tried for the murder of his wife, and was asked if he wished to say anything. After a pause, he said, 'She has driven me to destruction; I have five times attempted to destroy myself; three times to drown myself in the mill dam, and I have cut myself in the arm.'

28 DECEMBER **1842** An inquest was held at Gosport on James Robinson, who had been knocked down by horses drawing an omnibus two days earlier. The wheels ran over his neck, and he was killed at once. According to witnesses, the vehicle must have been driving at nearly eight miles per hour, and was in the act of turning the corner of a crowded thoroughfare at the time. A witness, who had known Robinson, said he was aged about 60, was deaf and suffered from poor eyesight. She watched him crossing the road; thinking that the driver was going too fast, she asked him to stop, but he took no notice. Another witness said he heard a passenger urge the driver not to stop after the accident lest he would be late for his train. The omnibus proprietor, Andrew Nance, said that James Boswell, who had been driving, was a sober, honest and careful man, and perfectly competent, but like other drivers he was sometimes under considerable pressure to drive too fast in order to reach the train on time. A verdict of accidental death was recorded.

29 DECEMBER **1879** Brothers Henry and John Amey, orange vendors, were charged with setting fire to a stack of straw belonging to Henry Dear, a farmer at Headborne Worthy. At the county sessions later that week, a boy of 10, William Henry Blake, said he had been at Worthy, where he bought an orange from them. His cousin Walter saw Henry Amey, who asked him the way to the village, and was given directions across the fields. A shepherd saw the prisoners as they came past the straw heap, within thirty yards of it, and five minutes later it was in flames. Another shepherd noticed them immediately after it had caught light, and saw they were walking very fast. Henry Blake, Mr Dear's foreman and Walter's father, saw Henry and accused him of starting the fire, but he denied it and became abusive. Both men were remanded in custody.

30 DECEMBER **1882** An inquest was held at Havant on the body of Barrett Boulton, a baby aged five months, son of Mr J.H. Boulton, a retired Assistant Paymaster with the Royal Navy, who lived at Bedhampton. The child had been in good health until his sudden death on 26 December. When Stewart Norman, the surgeon, carried out a post-mortem he said he could find no distinct cause of death. From the symptoms described to him, however, he thought the deceased had probably had a spasm of the windpipe, which would leave no trace after death. The jury recorded a verdict of death from natural causes.

1907   Major Coates Phillips, who had served with distinction in the South African War, committed suicide at Fleet. About two years previously, just after they had begun to live apart, his wife began divorce proceedings against him, but before the case was heard, he broke into her house and assaulted her. She took him to court but he continued to annoy her with threats, and she was granted a divorce. At the same time, an injunction was granted by which he was debarred from visiting her home or ever annoying her in any way. Despite this, he went to her house in December 1906 and attempted to kill himself in the conservatory. He was brought before the magistrates and committed to the Quarter Sessions, where he was bound over for twelve months after pledging himself never to go near his wife again. **31 DECEMBER**

The twelve months expired on New Year's Eve. In the evening Mrs Coates Phillips, her mother Mrs Lucine, and Mrs Philips's solicitor Mr Smith all met at her house to discuss business matters. At midnight Major Phillips, in a very excited state, pushed his way into the house, and fired at them. The bullet struck Mrs Lucine in the face. Mr Smith rushed forward to grapple with him, but before he could do so he received a bullet in the lower part of the body. Looking for somewhere to hide, Mrs Phillips and their small daughter ran across the hall and into a small closet underneath the stairs. The major ran after her, opened the door, and found her crouching on the ground in a corner. Standing over her, he fired again: this time the bullet missed her and entered the ground near her head. She collapsed with shock. He then shot himself through the right temple and fell dead across the cellar entrance. Mrs Lucine was taken to hospital, but later died of her injuries.

BIBLIOGRAPHY

BOOKS

Brode, Anthony, *Haunted Hampshire*, Countryside, 1981
Chambers, James, *The Norman Kings*, Weidenfeld & Nicolson, 1981
Clark, Richard, *Women and the Noose: A History of Female Execution*, Tempus, 2007
Eddleston, John J., *The Encyclopedia of Executions*, John Blake, 2004
Fielding, Steve, The *Hangman's Record, Vol. 1, 1868-1899; Vol. 2, 1900-1929; Vol. 3, 1930-1964*, CBD, 1994-2005
Hallam, Jack, *The Haunted Inns of England*, Wolfe, 1972
Oxford Dictionary of National Biography
Seymour, William, *Battles in Britain, 1066-1746*, Sidgwick & Jackson, 1979
Sly, Nicola, *Hampshire Murders*, History Press, 2009

NEWSPAPERS AND JOURNALS

Caledonian Mercury
Daily News
Hampshire Advertiser
Hampshire Telegraph & Sussex Chronicle
Illustrated Police News
The Morning Chronicle
The Pall Mall Gazette
Reynolds's Newspaper
The Times

HANGED AT WINCHESTER 1868-1963

On 24 December 1867, Frederick Baker [*see* 24 August 1867, p.105] became the last convicted murderer to be hanged in public at Winchester Gaol. All subsequent executions were held in private. Twenty-nine other men, some of whom committed their crimes outside Hampshire, have gone to the gallows at the same place, namely:

16.11.1874 Thomas Smith*
11.2.1878 James Caffyn
31.5.1878 Albert Brown*
31.5.1886 James Whelan
27.3.1888 George Clarke
25.8.1891 Edward Fawcett
6.8.1893 George Mason
18.7.1894 Samuel Elkins
12.12.1894 Cyrus Knight
12.12.1894 William Rogers
21.7.1896 Philip Matthews*
21.7.1896 Frederick Burden*
21.7.1896 Samuel Smith
18.7.1899 Charles Maidment*
22.7.1902 William Churcher*
16.12.1903 William Brown
16.12.1903 Thomas Cowdrey
26.12.1913 Augustus Penny
16.6.1914 Walter White
29.3.1917 Leo O'Donnell
19.8.1922 Thomas Allaway
30.7.1924 Abraham Goldenberg*
12.8.1926 Charles Finden*
22.4.1930 William Podmore*
28.7.1949 Sydney Chamberlain
7.7.1950 Zbigniew Gower
9.5.1951 William Shaughnessy
14.5.1959 Michael Tatum
17.12.1963 Dennis Whitty

* Denotes a case referred to in this book

Other titles published by The History Press

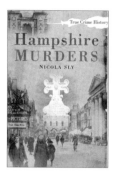

Hampshire Murders
NICOLA SLY

The grisly cases in this book include the killing of 'Sweet Fanny Adams' in 1867; the horrific murder committed by the postmaster at Grayshott in 1901; the mysterious poisoning of Hubert Chevis in 1943; and the gun battle in the village of Kingsclere in 1944, which resulted in the deaths of three people. Nicola Sly's carefully researched, well-illustrated and enthralling text will appeal to anyone interested in the shady side of Hampshire's history.

978 0 7509 5106 7

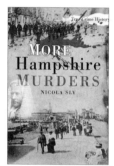

More Hampshire Murders
NICOLA SLY

In this follow-up to *Hampshire Murders*, forensic and legal psychologist Nicola Sly brings together more murderous tales that shocked not only the county but made headline news throughout the nation. They include the last recorded fatal duel to have been fought in England in 1845; the 1888 killing of Annie Vaughan by her stepfather who, for more than two years, had treated her 'as his wife'; and the 'murder that never was' – the victim's death was recorded as having been caused by his drunkenness until his naval commanding officer later confessed to killing him.

978 0 7524 5495 5

Hanged at Winchester
STEVE FIELDING

For decades, the high walls of Winchester Prison have contained some of the country's most infamous criminals. Until hanging was abolished in the 1960s it was also the main centre of execution for those convicted in Hampshire. Fully illustrated with photographs, news cuttings and engravings, *Hanged at Winchester* is sure to appeal to true-crime fans everywhere.

978 0 7524 5707 9

Haunted Hampshire
RUPERT MATTHEWS

This book showcases almost 100 ghostly encounters from around Hampshire. Arranged as a tour through the New Forest, Winchester, Southampton, the edge of the Downs, the Test Valley and the hills around Overton, you will discover ghostly seamen haunting the King's Bastion at Portsmouth, spirits of the Roundheads galloping through Crondall and a haunted megalith at Mottistone. Exploring everything from pubs and churchyards to castles and ports, *Haunted Hampshire* will appeal to everyone with an interest in the supernatural history of the area.

978 0 7524 4862 6

Visit our website and discover thousands of other History Press books.

www.thehistorypress.co.uk